IN THE SAME ORIGINAL FORMAT, GENERAL EDITOR AND DESIGNER DAVID BROWER:

This Is the American Earth, by Ansel Adams and Nancy Newhall
Words of the Earth, by Cedric Wright
These We Inherit: The Parklands of America, by Ansel Adams
"In Wildness Is the Preservation of the World," by Eliot Porter
The Place No One Knew: Glen Canyon on the Colorado, by Eliot Porter
The Last Redwoods: Photographs and Story of a Vanishing Scenic Resource, by
    Philip Hyde and Francois Leydet
Ansel Adams: A Biography. Volume I: The Eloquent Light, by Nancy Newhall
Time and the River Flowing: Grand Canyon, by Francois Leydet
Gentle Wilderness: The Sierra Nevada, text from John Muir,
    photographs by Richard Kauffman
Not Man Apart: Photographs of the Big Sur Coast,
    with lines from Robinson Jeffers
The Wild Cascades: Forgotten Parkland, by Harvey Manning,
    with lines from Theodore Roethke
Everest: The West Ridge, by Thomas F. Hornbein, with
    photographs from the American Mount Everest Expedition
Summer Island: Penobscot Country, by Eliot Porter
Navajo Wildlands: As Long as the Rivers Shall Run, photographs by
    Philip Hyde, text by Stephen Jett, edited by Kenneth Brower
Kauai and the Park Country of Hawaii, by Robert Wenkam
    edited by Kenneth Brower
Glacier Bay: The Land and the Silence, by Dave Bohn
Baja California and the Geography of Hope, photographs by Eliot Porter,
    text by Joseph Wood Krutch, edited by Kenneth Brower
Central Park Country: A Tune Within Us, photographs by Nancy and Retta
    Johnston, text by Mireille Johnston, introduction by Marianne Moore
Galapagos: The Flower of Wildness (both volumes edited by Kenneth Brower)
1. *Discovery,* photographs by Eliot Porter, introduction by Loren Eiseley,
    with selections from Charles Darwin, Herman Melville, and others; and
2. *Prospect,* photographs by Eliot Porter, introduction by John P. Milton,
    text by Eliot Porter and Kenneth Brower

THE EARTH'S WILD PLACES
Maui: The Last Hawaiian Place, by Robert Wenkam,
    edited, with Kipahulu Sketches, by Kenneth Brower
Return to the Alps, by Max Knight and Gerhard Klammet,
    edited, with selections from Alpine literature, by David R. Brower
The Primal Alliance, Earth and Ocean, by John Hay and Richard Kauffman,
    edited by Kenneth Brower
Earth and the Great Weather: The Brooks Range, by Kenneth Brower
Eryri, the Mountains of Longing, by Amory Lovins,
    with photographs by Philip Evans, edited by David R. Brower
A Sense of Place: The Artist and the American Land, by Alan Gussow,
    with illustrations by fifty-nine painters, and foreword by Richard Wilbur
Micronesia: Island Wilderness, by Kenneth Brower and Robert Wenkam
Guale, the Golden Coast of Georgia, James P. Valentine, Robert Hanie,
    Eugene Odom, John P. Milton *et al.,* edited by Kenneth Brower

Along the arc of the Georgia coast, from the mouth of the Savannah River to that of the St. Mary's, there is a chain of sea islands. On their eastern shores the white surf of the Atlantic rolls ceaselessly, and behind them lie the still waters of inland channels, stretches of quiet marsh, and the mainland.

. . .

Two great rivers flow into the sounds between these islands—the Ogeechee, not far from the Savannah, and the Altamaha, a little more than halfway down the coast. The Altamaha, the nobler stream, is formed by the junction of the Ocmulgee and the Oconee, which rise in northern Georgia. A broad and beautiful river as it nears the sea, its banks are bordered by a dense growth of live oak and cypress, magnolia and bay, all swathed in a tangled cobweb of floating gray moss; and on either bank, beyond the tropical growth of the stream, endless pine forests rise from a thick undergrowth of scrub palmetto.

. . .

The islands are as densely wooded as the banks of the Altamaha, though here and there in the interiors are open savannas, covered with harsh wiregrass, where palmetto trees stand, clean cut against the burning blue of the Southern sky. And where the land is low there are swamps, in which the spreading knees of the cypress are like Indian tepees, reflected in the wine-dark water. The woods are filled with the fragrance of myrtle, bay, and jessamine, and the only sounds that break the stillness are the musical notes of birds and the murmur of the wind-surf in the pines.

—CAROLINE LOVELL

Sweet gum leaves, Middle Place Pond, Ossabaw Island

It is the most amiable Country of the Universe.

—SIR ROBERT MONTGOMERY

Photographs by James Valentine. Text by Robert Hanie, with an introduction by Eugene Odum and John P. Milton, foreword by David R. Brower, and selections from the writings of Rachel Carson, William Bartram, John McPhee, John and Mildred Teal, and others. Edited by Kenneth Brower.

Guale, the Golden Coast of Georgia

FRIENDS OF THE EARTH ⊕ SAN FRANCISCO, NEW YORK, LONDON, PARIS

A CONTINUUM BOOK / THE SEABURY PRESS NEW YORK

Of the people of the States that I have now passed, I best like the Georgians.
They have charming manners, and their dwellings are mostly larger and
better than those of adjacent States. However costly or ornamental
their homes or their manners, they do not, like those of the New Englander,
appear as the fruits of intense and painful sacrifice and training, but are
entirely divested of artificial weights and measures, and seem to pervade
and twine about their characters as spontaneous growths with the durability
and charm of living nature.

—JOHN MUIR

ACKNOWLEDGMENT. This book came about through the suggestions and assistance of Mrs. Clifford B. ("Sandy") West and her husband, Mr. and Mrs. Charles Wood, Nathaniel Frothingham, Ron Miles, Donald Scott, Bob Rischarde, the late James Hoyt, David Brower, John Milton, Bill Griffin, Frank Hood, the Georgia Power Company's Harold Mckenzie and Edwin Hatch, the Georgia Conservancy, and the Garden Club of Georgia. We are grateful to all whom we have quoted (with due attribution) for what their thinking will be contributing to Guale and places like it for years to come.

We are grateful for permission to reprint excerpts from the following: ¶ Atheneum, New York: *Portrait of an Island*, by Mildred and John Teal, 1964. ¶ Farrar, Straus and Giroux, New York: *Encounters with the Archdruid*, by John McPhee, 1971. ¶ H. Hamilton, London: *Deliverance*, by James Dickey, 1970. ¶ Harper and Row, New York: *The Atlantic Shore*, by John Hay and Peter Farb, 1966. ¶ Houghton Mifflin Company, Boston: *The Edge of the Sea*, by Rachel Carson, 1955. ¶ Little, Brown and Company, Boston: *The Golden Isles of Georgia*, by Caroline Couper Lovell. 1932; and *Life and Death of the Salt Marsh*, by John and Mildred Teal, 1969. ¶ The Macmillan Company, New York: *The Inside Passage*, by Anthony Bailey, 1965.

This Friends of the Earth/Seabury Press printing contains corrections of minor errors but no substantive changes in text, photographs, or other illustrations. For current information about what is happening in the earth's wild places, write Friends of the Earth, San Francisco.

LIBRARY OF CONGRESS CATALOG CARD NO. 74-17220.

ISBN 0-913890-02-2

Printed and bound in Italy

"The parrot of Carolina" (Mark Catesby)

Foreword

IN THE FIRST volume of the series, The Earth's Wild Places, Loren Eiseley was saying of the Galapagos Islands something that is quite pertinent to Georgia's islands:

"Voyages without islands to touch upon would be epics of monotony. Whether for diversion of thought or for the easing of the physical body, men demand periods, points of reference, islands fixed in the turbulence of giant waters, or, if eluding the compass, still haunting the mind."

Kenneth Brower, editor of the Galapagos work and of this one, saw further parallel:

"This is a book in praise of islands. Its two volumes are an investigation of the virtues of islands as points of reference, both scientific and poetic. They are concerned with islands as laboratories, refuges, genetic reservoirs, places for future discovery. The book arose from concern for islands and the fragile life forms they have evolved, the gentle insular wildness that is vanishing so rapidly around the world. Its concern is both for oceanic islands like the Galapagos, and for islands isolated in other ways—for islands of life, like the very small North American island of whooping cranes, a last island of common genes and nesting calls, or like the limited fraternity of the Indian rhinoceros, or that of the fresh-water seals of Lake Baikal. Its plea is for diversity, for all possible variety, animate and inanimate, in the texture of our planet's surface."

About a sign in a zoo alluding to endangered species and "the final emptiness of extinction," he added:

"We don't need more emptiness in the world—there is presently a surfeit of that. We need to celebrate the opposite of emptiness, and this book is the first in a series that will attempt to do this, to point out the fullness and variousness of the earth's wild places.

"A living planet is a rare thing, perhaps the rarest in the universe, and a very tenuous experiment at best. We need all the company we can get on our unlikely journey. . . . The more varied the life the better. There is no requirement that our voyage be a monotonous one."

That was in 1968, in between Thor Heyerdahl's voyages across the Atlantic, the first one on an essentially clean Atlantic, the second, ten years later, finding him for forty-three days out of the fifty-seven making his way through petrochemical detritus. That was before the Apollo voyages had shown, first from the moon, then from other planets, how rare our living planet really is. Had Neanderthal Man left the earth in his age at the speed of an Apollo, he would not yet have reached the next nearest sun that might conceivably have a living planet.

This is indeed the only earth, and there is no spare. There are very clear limits and they are very clearly, we see now, being exceeded. The part of the earth man has already touched—sometimes gently and sometimes brutally—can sustain his progress if he applies his science, his technology, and his genius to the challenge of going back over what he has touched and healing his mistakes. Hardly a tenth of that earth is still essentially unimpaired by his technology. Most of the impairment of the rest of the earth has happened in the last fraction of a second of the Week of Creation, in which life began at noon on Tuesday and in which it is now Saturday midnight. The part of the earth that has been spared is the wilderness, the living web of life that shaped all life, including ours, for all but that last fraction of a second. Wilderness is an increasingly rare thing that civilization's new-found fascination with Growth can overrun swiftly, but to no appreciable avail, and the world would be a cage without that wilderness. We can tear the miracle of wilderness apart but we cannot reassemble it, and the vestige that too few people know about is all that all people will ever have to inform them. "Wilderness," Nancy Newhall has said so well, "holds answers to questions man has not yet learned how to ask."

Man could explode across the land, but only at the expense of the diversity essential to the only world he can live upon. When a wild population, such as of beaver, explodes, the beaver overload their range,

Beached buoy, Cumberland

become neurotic, lose vitality, and starve. Mankind has a range too, and it has a maximum carrying capacity consistent with a good life—a life with enough resources on hand to serve a restrained humanity and to spare nations from the final quarrel over what is in the bottom of the cornucopia a few have emptied so swiftly. Jerry Mander, who wrote the advertisement that spoiled the Sierra Club's tax status but helped save Grand Canyon, epitomized what needs to happen now in a subsequent Sierra Club advertisement. It filled a page and a half in *The New York Times* early in 1969 and began, "Before it is too late, we should like to preserve Earth as a 'conservation district' within the Universe, a sort of Earth National Park." Mr. Mander was concerned not so much for nature, which would pretty much take care of itself, but rather for man, whose attempt to exceed natural limits is self-defeating. He realized, with Paul Sears, that "as we lengthen and elaborate the chain of technology that intervenes between us and the natural world, we forget that we become steadily more vulnerable to even the slightest failure in that chain."

One step toward treating Earth itself as a national park is to place special parts of it in a sort of Earth International Park, in a World Heritage envisioned by Russell Train when he was president of the Conservation Foundation. The World Heritage would encompass scenic resources of importance to the world as a whole, such as the Grand Canyon, the redwoods, and the Serengeti; it would also be concerned with cultures, monuments, and ecological uniqueness. The nations to which the world heritage belonged would retain all control, but the rest of the world would help financially, if need be, and coöperate in preserving and interpreting. The 1972 United Nations Conference on the Human Environment, thanks to the leadership of Russell Train and many others, declared their approval of the World Heritage and the United Nations subsequently approved it. The United States has signed the convention.

Guale, the Golden Coast of Georgia, exists because we believe the region it describes belongs in the World Heritage. How, through what various good offices, can the world as a whole help preserve it? How can the costs and responsibilities of sparing and understanding this region be shared? How can it combine governmental and private conservation, and how can what is joined here be put together similarly in other lands? And in time?

We seek suggestions and action. Perhaps a World Heritage Fund is needed, patterned after the World Wildlife Fund, to provide a steady source of revenue to countries caring for the heritage. Or an international tourist tuition. A particular role in interpreting places belongs to those who have lived there, and who can best become the teachers in a literally open university. A new kind of private conservation could let individuals purchase wildness and cede their development rights to a government that would not otherwise get around to protecting it soon enough. Somewhere, on one of the islands off Georgia's coast, or on a threshold to those islands, let there be meetings every year of people who care especially about both threshold and island. Let the meetings search out the steps toward achieving for Guale, as best they can, what Theodore Roosevelt had in mind when he said on Grand Canyon's rim; "Leave it as it is. You cannot improve on it. The ages have been at work on it and man can only mar it." True, there is no Grand Canyon in Guale, but neither is there a Guale in or near the Grand Canyon. In both places, and in other great places around the world, there is still an opportunity to discern what belongs there and to avoid the things man might wish to add that don't belong. Kenneth Brower, John Earl, Robert Hanie, John P. Milton, Eugene Odom, James Valentine, and many friends here and gone have joined to let us know what really does belong, and we are most grateful, and grateful as well to the generous people who helped them.

Let each progressive move toward a new understanding of the living landscape, of which we are inseparably a part, be duly celebrated. May Guale and the golden coast of Georgia always celebrate our having acted in behalf of people who have not yet arrived on earth, and celebrate it by being as beautiful for them as it is to us!

DAVID R. BROWER, *President*

Friends of the Earth

Berkeley, California, May 24, 1974

Introduction

WORLD HERITAGE

Twenty-five hundred years ago the Chinese sage Lao-Tsu wrote:

> *The universe is sacred.*
> *You cannot improve it.*
> *If you try to change it*
> *   you will ruin it.*
> *If you try to hold it*
> *   you will lose it.*

Guale, the golden coast, cannot be improved upon. Neither can it be grasped and held firm in the hand of civilization. This coast is a living, dynamic thing, constantly changing with each pulse of the marsh tides, each storm that batters the island forests, each shift of ocean current that erodes one shoreline and builds up another. The challenge to man here is to respect the wilderness the coast contains, to learn to leave it as it is. The rhythms of the sea, the tides, the marsh, and the forest have much to teach, but first we must stop improving, stop grasping, stop being hypnotized by the rhythms of machine-made consciousness.

On the islands of Jekyll and Tybee, parks for mass tourism have been established. Many of Jekyll's dunes have been obliterated to make way for parking lots, shopping centers, motels, and fancy restaurants. Housing subdivisions, roads, bridges, airport facilities, and golf courses have carved up a great deal of the island's forest. Large areas of adjacent salt marsh have been drained and dredged for marinas and yacht basins. Jekyll was one of the wild islands I lived on during my first trip to the Georgia coast, and recently I visited the island again. I remembered how it had been twenty years before, when the island landscape was still intact. I recalled the stretches of wild ocean beach where loggerhead turtles heaved themselves onshore during warm June nights, and I remembered the shadowed trails through arching forests of live oak, Spanish moss draping the limbs in soft, hanging clouds. Occasionally the curtains of color swayed gently with the wind. Green spears of palmetto were the only sharpness in a forest of softened edges.

We have made some progress in learning how to let the coast alone. State legislation has been passed to protect the salt marsh from development, federal and state controls on industrial pollution are receiving increasing support, and some of the barrier islands have been preserved. Wassaw and Blackbeard Islands are set aside as National Wildlife Refuges; Big Cumberland Island is on the way to becoming a National Seashore; Sapelo Island is managed in part by the State as a game management area, and in part by the Sapelo Island Research Foundation as a study area; Wolf Island is held as a preserve by the Nature Conservancy; and the privately held islands of St. Catherine, Ossabaw, and Little Cumberland all are owned by people who have exceptional concern for environmental protection.

The difficulty with actions taken so far to protect the Georgia Coast is that they are piecemeal, while the coast is a unified whole. Any changes detrimental to one part will ultimately cause effects throughout the entire living fabric, so that planning to protect the region's organic wholeness requires a large view. Recently, a more holistic vision of the coast has been furthered by a recognition that it is an area of great national and international significance.

Over the past few years, a number of environmental leaders in Georgia have sought to include the Golden Coast as one of the first areas designated for the World Heritage. These efforts have resulted in considerable international interest and support. In addition, the State of Georgia has recently initiated its own "Georgia Heritage Trust," a farsighted effort designed to stem the alarmingly rapid loss of endangered natural and cultural sites in Georgia.

The coast of Georgia is unique among the coasts of the world. There are other long, white-sand beaches in the world, of course, and from New Jersey to Florida to the gulf coast of Texas there are similar barrier islands. There is estuarine marsh at Chesapeake Bay and elsewhere along the Atlantic Coast (though the marsh grasses of Georgia *do* grow taller and richer than any). There is subtropical vegetation elsewhere in the subtropics, naturally. But nowhere else do these things come together in one place. No place on earth has such a diversity of subtropical coastal life and landscape. It is in the combination that the uniqueness resides, and the uniqueness qualifies the Georgia coast for inclusion in the World Heritage.

—JOHN P. MILTON
President, Threshold Inc.

May, 1973

Maush Sparrow

ant Gose

m of Florida

LIVING MARSH

It was in 1954 that I first really saw the Georgia barrier-island salt-marsh estuary. Before this time I had often viewed the vast expanses of salt marsh and winding waterways from the causeways at Savannah and Brunswick, sensing something of the mysterious forces at work. I had been on the beaches of several of the Golden Isles and had watched birds from various vantage points, often during the field-trip meetings of the Georgia Ornithological Society. I recall standing enthralled with the display of color and sound of Painted Buntings among the moss-festooned live oaks on an early May morning. I remember cruising up and down the Savannah River estuary in quest of shorebirds with the late Ivan Tomkins, Savannah's greatest naturalist of this century. All of this, however, was viewing from the outside, admiring the sweep and the spectacle of the landscape. It was like being impressed with the color, contour, and movement of a wild animal without inquiring—or, perhaps, not caring—about its insides, or how it functions, or how it survives. But in 1954, in the company of colleagues and students, I peeked into the insides of the estuarine system for the first time.

The revelation, so to speak, came shortly after the late R. J. Reynolds, Jr. had invited the University of Georgia to establish a research laboratory on Sapelo Island, which he then owned and which was later to be acquired by the state. We were in the process of assembling a small staff of newly minted Ph.D.s and eager graduate students, setting up a laboratory in an unused, but substantially built dairy barn, and exploring the environment that was to be our outdoor laboratory, or Research Park, the term we now use to promote the idea of preserving large natural areas for ecological research.

We moved up tidal creeks in small outboard motorboats on ebbing tides. As the water rushed by and the

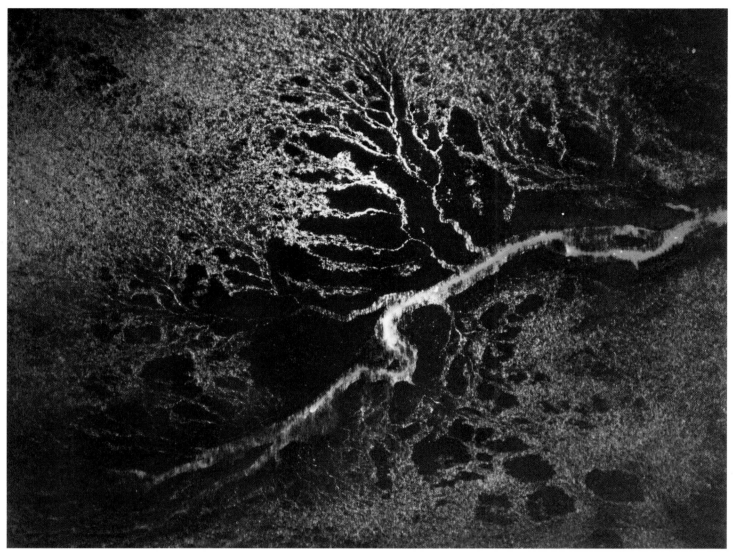

Marsh, Tybee

boats sank lower, we found ourselves in deep canyons of golden mud banks (the color, as we were to learn later, due to immense populations of diatoms and other algae), topped by six-foot high stands of marsh grass looking for all the world like a well-fertilized stand of sugar cane. Samples of the outrushing water revealed a heavy load of suspended matter which most people would call mud, but which on closer inspection, proved to contain large amounts of organic detritus (particulate organic matter rich in vitamins and calories). The notion came to us, in those early days, that we were in the arteries of a remarkable energy-absorbing natural system whose heart was the pumping action of the tides. The entire tideland complex of barrier islands, marshes, creeks, and river mouths was a single operational unit linked together by the tide. If we were right, each part of the system would have to be dependent for its life-sustaining energy not only on the direct rays of the sun, but also on the energy of the tides. Could it be, we asked, that organisms in this environment have not only evolved to become adapted to the stresses of this energetic environment, but have learned (through natural selection) how to convert some of the tidal energy to useful metabolism for their own advantage? Does nature routinely exploit tidal power as men have dreamed of doing for centuries? In the past biologists who studied estuarine and seashore organisms had been preoccupied with how such life adapts to the obvious stresses; that some of the stresses might be converted to subsidies was, and still is, something of a new theory. This germ of an idea, subsequently developed by twenty years of team research on Sapelo, will, we hope, provide the basis for man to design with, rather than against, nature on this remarkable sea coast.

Once the general concept of a naturally subsidized ecosystem emerged, the research program at Sapelo automatically fell in place. It was not necessary to set up any kind of rigid research program or priority schedule because everyone who came to work at Sapelo, staff and students alike, soon became caught up in the excitement of the energy-flow approach. It was fortunate that we had about fifteen years for quiet, unpressured study before the need for land-use decisions became acute enough to require that our basic findings be applied. The funds provided by Mr. Reynolds through his Sapelo Research Foundation enabled us to work on whatever we thought important in trying to understand the system just the way it is without having to justify, at least for the time being, what we were doing in terms of man's needs. I think we can now document how such independent study does in the long run provide the basis for the most practical of decisions.

The "plumbing" of the system—the water flow—was one of the first aspects to receive our attention. Hydrology studies were started by Robert Ragotskie, the first Director of the Marine Institute. Because the tidal amplitude is high in Georgia, five to eight feet between low and high tide, the magnitude of volumes and currents of water that move twice daily in and out is astounding, and impressed us all. It is a dominating force that links the parts of the system on a very short time scale. Later we came to use the term "fluctuating water-level ecosystem" for this kind of natural order. The Everglades with its annual "tides," draw-down fish ponds, and rice paddies are other places where the rise and fall of water are vital to the maintenance and productivity of certain species. The great power in Georgia's tides is the most important thing to remember when it comes to practical matters of land management. Terrestrial man, accustomed to *terra firma*, tends neither to understand the dynamism nor appreciate the beauty of fluctuating ecosystems. He tends to want to confront the forces with artificial barriers and try to stabilize the environment, because it's often inconvenient when the landscape doesn't stand still, especially to a race of men with a strong property-owning ethic. But confronting high energy forces head-on requires a great deal of money, as the public, and even powerful governmental agencies like the Army Engineers, who are sometimes nourished too much by pork barrel politics, are beginning to realize. And more important, blocking or stabilizing the flow removes the useful energy input along with the stressful, resulting in an immediate decline in productivity. The energy-absorbing system then becomes an energy-blocking system that is vulnerable to erosion and washouts when storms come. The idea is dawning that it just might be cheaper and maybe even better to design with the grain rather than against it.

From the onset I was interested in the community ecology of the stands of marsh grass. There was a succession of graduate students, beginning with Alfred Smalley, who developed strong leg muscles wading around in the muddy jungles of marsh grass in order to earn degrees. The general pattern of primary production, the major food chains, and the population ecology of key animals such as snails, grasshoppers, and marsh wrens were worked out in these early days. John Teal, one of the first resident staff members, carried out important experiments with fiddler crabs and other creatures of the mud and sand, and he published the first energy budget for the marsh as a whole. Later, John and his wife Mildred were to write widely read books on the marsh and the natural and human lore of the Georgia Sea Islands. We are constantly amending Teal's energy budget as new information comes in, and we still have much to learn. About the only difference between then and now is that our tools have become more sophisticated. The first generation of students relied on meter sticks, clippers, buckets, shovels, and the like; the present generation is making use of new technology associated with remote sensing, tracers, spectrometric chemistry, electron microscopy, and computers.

To the botanical specialist, the Georgia salt marshes seem at first glance very dull, because only one kind of plant, *Spartina alterniflora*, the salt marsh cord grass, is immediately visible. It would take only a few minutes to collect a specimen, press it, and go home. In truth there are hundreds of species of green plants when we consider the diatoms, the green algae, the blue-green algae, the dinoflagellates, and others that inhabit the marsh water and live in an almost continuous blanket in the sediments. But botanists don't generally deal with these kinds of plants, of course, usually leaving them for the microbiologist. There are other kinds of vascular plants, including other marsh grasses, salicornias, composites, and shrubs that occupy the border country between the *S. alterniflora* marsh and the more elevated terrain. And there are still other interesting plants, including other species in the genus Spartina, that occupy the sand dunes and the brackish- and fresh-water marshes of the river mouth sections of the estuary. Yet it is *Spartina alterniflora* that is of primary interest to the ecologist, because it is uniquely able to cope with tides and salt, and in Georgia it contributes from fifty to eighty per cent (depending on locality) of the total primary production on which most animals and other consumers in the whole estuary depend. Few of the consumers eat marsh grass on the stalk, but many depend directly or indirectly on its tissues after they have decomposed and are enriched in a unique microbial food factory powered by the tides and other water currents.

It did not take us very long to find out that this one species formed by no means a uniform population, but existed in distinct varieties or ecotypes, which, in growth form, production potential, and animal associates differ as greatly as do many distinct species in, say, an upland meadow. We have found it convenient to recognize three kinds of stands:

1. The tall Spartina streamside stands that border the marsh creeks. Mature stalks grow 3-4 meters (9 feet or more) along the banks. In better locations they number about 40 per square meter, with, depending on the season, a varying number (up to 140 per square meter) of smaller, understory stalks.

2. The medium Spartina middle marsh stands in the vast interior where creeks break up in a dendritic pattern and dead-end. Similar stands also grow on far sides of stream banks (natural levees). Here mature stalks measure 1-2 meters (3-6 feet) and number 60 or so per square meter with numerous small understory stalks.

3. Short Spartina stands on the high marsh, reached only by high spring tides, or in stagnant lower areas where tidal irrigation is also less frequent. Here stalks are small, 0.4 to 1 meter (1-3 feet), but numerous, up to 200 or more per square meter.

Our most recent estimates of the annual net production of the three zones is shown (in round figures) in the table. Also shown is an estimate, for comparison, of a *Spartina cynosuroides* stand growing in the brackish or fresh water along coastal rivers. Remember that by net production we mean the organic matter available to the rest of the community after the plants have respired what they need for their maintenance.

COMPARISON OF ANNUAL NET PRODUCTIVITY

| | Dry weight | |
	gms/M²	Tons/acre
Spartina alterniflora†		
Tall grass, streamside stands	4000	17.8
Medium grass, middle marsh stands	2300	10.2
Short grass, high marsh stands	750	3.3
Spartina cynosuroides†		
Tall grass, riverbank stands	2000	8.9
Sugar cane, Hawaii*	—	14.7
Corn, U.S.A.*	—	5.7
Corn, world average*	—	3.1

†These marsh grasses are in major habitat zones of Georgia coastal marshes.
*These crop productivity estimates are based on annual dry matter yields of the whole above-ground plant, not just the edible portion; thus, figures are comparable to those given for marsh grasses.

The difference between the productivity of the streamside stands that receive vigorous, daily tidal irrigation and the other stands that are less frequently or less vigorously flooded gives an indication of the extent to which Spartina grass is able to cope with and benefit by tidal energy. Where naturally subsidized in this manner, productivity equals or exceeds man's best agricultural crops (see table). Man's crops are also subsidized, of course, but by tractor fuel, fertilizers, and other things, all of which enable the plant to make maximum use of the sun. It is interesting to note that the very high yields now being obtained with the use of the new so-called miracle grains are the result of breeding not so much to improve ability to utilize sun energy, but to improve capacity to benefit from intensive cultivation and very heavy applications of chemicals (fertilizers, pesticides, herbicides). Man pays an increasingly high price for these crop subsidies, while all of the energy in the tidal marsh is free.

When we first reported that the Georgia salt marshes were very productive, we were not able to explain it fully. When one considers that high light intensity, high summer temperatures, high salinity, and the unstable substrate that is anaerobic (without oxygen) below the top few centimeters all tend to be metabolic drains on spermatophytic plants, it is a wonder that the marsh grass has any energy left to produce anything. The tidal subsidy is, of course, part of the answer, but it remained for a team of Australian plant biochemists to discover in 1966 that some kinds of grasses and a few nongrass species utilize a photosynthetic pathway that avoids almost entirely the photorespiration that burns up stored food reserves in ordinary plants when temperature, light and water become stressful. It turns out that Spartina grasses belong to this class of plant, now designated as C_4 type plants, in contrast to the more common C_3 types (the numbers referring to the number of carbon atoms in the first product of CO_2 fixation).

While the studies of marsh grass and its associated community were continuing apace, other investigators were fascinated with the other two major primary producers of the estuary, namely, the mud algae (benthic algae is the technical term) and the floating algae (phytoplankton). Lawrence Pomeroy devised an ingenious method to measure the total metabolism (photosynthesis and respiration) of intact mud algae, which color the creek banks and the floor of the marsh its greenish gold. He was able to place bell jars over the substrate and to measure the gas exchanges within them, both in the light and when covered. He found that these fixed microscopic plants contributed as much as a third of the total food-making activity of the inner and upper portions of the marsh-estuary. Especially interesting was the discovery that they function the year around at about the same rate—a good example of how a mixed, diverse population can compensate for seasonal changes in temperature and light. During the winter the algae collect near the surface and photosynthesize most actively when the tide is out and the sun warms the surface. In summer, they avoid the hot surfaces and are most active when the tide is in and their environment is water cooled. Richard Williams spent several years at Sapelo classifying and working out the details of various species in this remarkable group of plants. He found that some of the larger diatoms form tubes in the sediments, and move up and down them according to light, temperature, and tidal conditions. (Diatoms *are* plants, but some of them move with a mysterious gliding motion like that of a small flatworm.)

Ragotskie, Pomeroy, and Claire Schelske measured the production rates of the phytoplankton, or floating algae, finding that their contribution to overall productivity was more or less inversely related to the turbidity of the water. Thus the phytoplankton become more important in the deeper, clearer waters of the sounds and offshore areas.

All these different crops contribute to the richness of the whole tidal complex. The estuary and its marshes are a real multiculture. That the plant community is seasonally programmed, so that one or more components are active at any time of year, even in quite cold climates, is a major reason estuaries have a high annual productivity. In contrast, most of man's monoculture crops are active for only a part of the year; the daily or monthly rate of photosynthesis is impressive in them, but the annual rate may not be.

Pomeroy began a series of investigations that are still continuing on the behavior of mineral nutrients in the estuary. He found that the marsh is a nutrient trap that hoards and recycles such vital nutrients as phosphorus. The marsh grass and the sediments act both as a sink and a pump, meaning that large amounts of nutrients that come into the estuary from either sea or land are quickly stored, but become available on demand by organisms. The practical meaning of these findings is clear. The estuary is an effective tertiary treatment plant for mineral nutrients from man's systems. If man secondarily treats sewage from urban and recreational developments to remove the organic matter, which the marsh can not handle in large amounts, because of the large amount of natural organic matter already present, the estuary can function as a most efficient partner with him. Since tertiary treatment is very expensive if done in man's artificial systems, the estuary's ability to contain nutrients provides one of the most important economic reasons for preserving this environment in its natural state. Recently we have calculated that an acre of estuary can be worth $50,000 for its tertiary treatment of wastes; it would cost man this much in capital and maintenance to do this free work in artificial systems.

Although we knew that bacteria, fungi, and other microbes must be important in the food chain that domi-

nates the metabolism of the estuary, we were almost completely ignorant of what really goes on in all that lovely gunk that swishes around in the arteries of the system like so much life-giving blood. So we began looking around for a young microbiologist who might enlighten us. It was not easy to find anybody willing to shed his clean white coat and leave the comfort of an orderly laboratory. What microbiologist in his right mind would want to give up a tidy world of neat rows of test tubes, purring machines, and rows of lab assistants in order to tackle a real world of sediment? I once thought of writing an article, "The Green Mud and Other Stories," to drum up some enthusiasm. I note that Edward S. Deevey has recently scooped me with a delightful essay called "In Defense of Mud," published in the Bulletin of the Ecological Society.

We did find a young microbiologist, Ted Starr, who was willing to try. The year that Ted spent at Sapelo was an extremely frustrating one for him and us. We didn't have the fancy equipment that he was trained to work with, and none of us really had any idea how to begin. The first time we took Ted into the marsh he got out of the boat and immediately sank to his waist in mud—a most unfortunate introduction. We did learn two things that year. We found that the traditional pure-culture approach of microbiology is useless when it comes to natural systems; a whole new approach of *in situ* study had to be invented, an approach involving assays and measurements of by-products and actions on substrates. And Starr discovered that some of the marine bacteria were prolific producers of vitamin B_{12}.

It was about ten years before the microbiological world was really ready to open for us. The late Paul Burkholder and his wife, internationally known for their pioneer work in marine microbiology, did quite a bit of work at Sapelo in collaboration with students and associates. They measured decomposition rates of marsh grass and became especially interested in bacterial production of vitamins and other growth promoters and of antibiotics in the estuary (work that Starr had started). Their findings suggested that these substances might function as environmental hormones, regulating the system's metabolism in a manner analogous to the thyroid, pituitary, and adrenal hormones that regulate the human body. This theory is yet to be verified. Today microbial ecology is a new and booming subject. We have a whole host of enthusiastic investigators and students who are bringing new ideas and tools to the study of the important world of detritus.

The idea that estuaries are important nursery grounds

for seafood animals is a long-standing concept. Our work measured and further documented that the marshes not only provide protection and nourishment for the very young stages of shrimp and other seafood that spend the early part of their life cycles in the shallow water, but also export food into the deeper waters to support the older stages of this seafood as well as fish and shellfish of species that never come into the marsh itself. That the marshes support fisheries many miles downstream provides another compelling reason for preservation of the marshes. Other investigators have shown that sea grasses and mangroves are likewise important in supporting fisheries of other southern coastal regions where these species are the ecological equivalent of the salt grass.

We invited Japanese aquaculture specialists to come to Sapelo to determine if the Georgia estuaries could support the kind of intensive oyster culture for which Japan is noted. They found that the potential is there indeed, though it is not now economically feasible to carry out raft culture in the United States. We are a beef-eating people and not yet hungry enough to need seriously to invest in aquaculture. It's nice to know that the potential is there, however, and aquaculture is another reason for keeping the estuary healthy. We may one day need this source of protein.

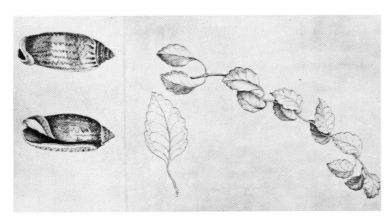

William Bartram: Southern arrow wood and netted olive shell

Closely related to studies on living components of sediments and suspended matter were geological studies, which received major emphasis in the Sapelo research program. Again, it was not easy at first to find geologists who were interested in sand and mud when there are so many fine mountains and good hard rocks to work with. We finally looked for talent in the Texas universities, where sedimentary geology is emphasized because of its importance to the oil industry. Over a period of years the late John Hoyt, Jim Henry, Jim Howard, and Oran Pilky investigated many aspects of beach, island, and marsh

formation. They proposed a completely new theory of the geological formation of Georgia's golden islands: that they may not be sea islands in the sense that they formed at sea, but may instead be remnants of the old coastline when the sea was at its lowest during the ice ages. The geological work verified that the islands, and their sand beaches and dunes, are, like the marshes, energy absorbing systems. They are constantly changed and shifted by the tides, storms, and longitudinal coastal currents. As in the marshes, it is important to distinguish between different ecological zones on the sea islands, especially when it comes to land use. The following zones are usually evident, starting with the ocean front and moving inland:

1. The active or unstable zone of sand beaches and dunes, which are constantly forming, shifting, and becoming colonized by such characteristic pioneer sand plants as sea oats (*Uniola paniculata*), sand grass (*Triplasis purpura*), sea purslane (*Sevuvium portulacastrum*), beach morning glory (*Ipomoea*, several species), beach croton (*Croton punctatus*), and beach euforbia (*Euforbia polygonifolia*).

2. The stabilized-dune zone comes next. Organic matter accumulates in the upper layers of these older dunes and woody plants such as wax myrtle, live oak, and juniper become established. The vegetation pins down the dunes and they cease to migrate. Freshwater ponds sometimes form between the dunes.

3. There is often, but not always, a slough with salt or brackish marsh that separates the dune area from the main body of the island. This area acts as a catch basin for any storm waters that may sweep over the dune area.

4. The main body of the island lies above the level of all but the most severe storm tides and supports magnificent forests of slash pine, live oak, magnolia, and many other species.

Again, the nature of these linked zones suggests a basis for prudent land use by man. The geological studies provide a very strong basis for recommended dos and don'ts. No rigid, substantial structures should be placed on the active zone for two reasons: (1) such structures will be subject to damage from storms, which will mean injury and grief for the residents, and huge "disaster relief" bills that all of us, as taxpayers, are called upon to bear, and (2) on the natural strand the energy of high tides and storms is dissipated gradually over large areas of yielding sand. Rigid structures, including sea walls, constructed to protect the inappropriate housing, deflect the energy of the water back on the beach, which then becomes rapidly eroded and steep. Thus any effort to protect structures placed too close to the ocean results eventually in degrading the beach, the very resource that people built there to enjoy. Houses, apartments, and condominiums, if they must be built, should be built only on stabilized land, and preferably up on pilings so storm water can flow under without harm to anything.

The word "estuary" is derived from the root *aestus*, which means "tide." A textbook would define an estuary as: "a semi-enclosed coastal body of water which has a free connection with the open sea; it is thus strongly affected by tidal action, and within it sea water is mixed, and usually measureably diluted, with fresh water from land drainage." (The textbook in this case is my own.) There are many kinds of estuaries and they have different features that bear importantly on man's use and management. From the standpoint of a hydrologist, estuaries vary from those dominated by rivers where the lighter fresh water overflows the heavier salt, forming a two-layered "salt-wedge" to those dominated by the sea, where stratification is horizontal rather than vertical; the Georgia estuaries are largely of the latter type. Estuaries can also be classified geomorphologically, or according to "land form." Estuaries in Norway and British Columbia are the "fjord-type"—deep valleys carved out by glaciers. Other estuaries, like San Francisco Bay, are formed by geological faulting or other tectonic processes. Still other estuaries are drowned river valleys, like Chesapeake Bay. Finally, there are barrier-island, coastal-plain estuaries, or "bar-built estuaries," like those of Georgia. In these the water moves in great sheets over long distances. They are energy-absorbing systems, and this is the key to understanding and management.

Public awareness of the unique nature of Georgia's coastal zone and ensuing conservation action came with dramatic suddenness in 1968. It was triggered when a large industrial company requested that the state lease marshlands near Savannah for strip mining of the phosphate beds that lie below the marshes. The Governor requested that the University System of Georgia set up a commission of experts to study the situation and make a recommendation. A thorough study was made, including not only environmental, mining, and geological considerations, but also a detailed economic cost-benefit study by the University's business school. We were able to provide important baseline data from our long years of study at Sapelo. The final report was, in effect, an objective impact study of the type now required by federal law (the National Environmental Protection Act). It showed rather clearly that the proposed mining was not a good deal for the state, either environmentally or economically. As a result, the lease request was denied. The

report also recommended that a permanent state commission be set up to deal with such matters.

Tremendous public interest was generated by the incident. Stories, editorials, and feature articles appeared in newspapers throughout the state, and there were feature spreads in *Life*, *Time*, and other national magazines. The momentum for a state act to protect the Georgia marshes began to build. A young state senator from Brunswick,

Reed Harris, introduced such a bill in the state legislature. For a while it remained locked up in committee, but public interest was so great that it had to come out. In the space of about six months, editorials, cartoons, Sunday supplements, national magazine publicity, a flood of letters to legislators, constructive student activism, input from the scientific community, unified support from conservation organizations, fact sheets widely distributed to schools and citizens, bumper stickers and buttons ("save Georgia's marshes") all played a part in changing the attitude of a whole state and convincing its legislators that natural resources need protective legislation and the establishment of broadly based statewide control agencies. The result was the near unanimous passage in 1970 of a strong marshland protection act, despite intense political opposition by a few, but powerful, vested interests. I recall a sequence of headlines and editorials that went something as follows: "Save the Marshes"; "Filling the

Georgia marshes would be as senseless as filling the San Francisco Bay"; "Students in drive to save marshes"; "House majority whip switches sides, backs marshland bill"; "Marshland bill passes in senate"; "Bill to guard marshes sent to Governor"; "The system works on Marshland Bill." The latter editorial pointed out what we all must remember: the legislative system works when there is a strong public mood for decision; and this mood must have a rational basis if legislative action is to have a long-term effect. In retrospect, I believe it was the concepts of energy absorption and productivity, as outlined in this narrative, which provided the rational basis here.

Sentiment in Georgia and elsewhere is building for a similar protection act for the active beach and dune zone. Ecological principles are being increasingly used as a basis for planning for recreational development on the sea islands and industrial development on the mainland, by both state and private interests. But there is yet much to be done.

The photographs in this book are portraits of the bits and pieces of a single ecological system. All the pieces do fit together, and they all play a part. Two civilizations, the Indians and the plantation-makers, have come and gone, and now a new industrial civilization is moving in. Only if there is general public awareness of the need to preserve the integrity of the natural landscape can we hope to blunt the pressures for inappropriate development, and plan for a full partnership of man and nature—for mutual benefit.

On Sapelo Island we had fifteen years to learn about the marsh before any practical application of our findings was necessary. In another fifteen years we will have still more knowledge, and more applications. If we had not had the first fifteen years, and a wild marsh to work in, we would not have learned what we did, and the marsh might have died without our knowing what we had lost. "Wilderness," Nancy Newhall has written, "holds answers to questions man has not yet learned how to ask." Not the least of the virtues of the Georgia marsh, I like to think, is that it gave us the time and the place and the peace to study the virtues of it.

—Eugene P. Odum
Director, Institute of Ecology
The University of Georgia

May, 1973

DYING RIVERS

Loading the canoe, I had not really been aware of the water, but now I was. It felt profound, its motion built into it by the composition of the earth for hundreds of miles upstream and down, and by thousands of years. The standing there was so good, so fresh and various and continuous, so vital and uncaring around my genitals, that I hated to leave it.

—James Dickey

Three ancient rivers, the Altamaha, the Savannah, and the Ogeechee, flow, as they have flowed for almost always, to Guale.

For 280 million years the Altamaha has run across Georgia to the sea. The river was one hundred miles longer during Pliocene time, when the shoreline was way out there; it was shorter in the time of the Pleistocene glaciers, and now once again it is extending itself. Daily the Altamaha delivers a billion gallons of living water to the sea, and together with the Savannah it carries nutrients and sediments vital to the marshlands of coastal Georgia. The river was the avenue up which white men moved into the virgin red cypress swamps and into the great virgin slash pine forest that covered the coastal plain. They erected sawmill towns at Darien and Doctortown and Lumber City, and the towns hummed day and night; it is said that by the 1870s you could walk four miles on the river without getting your feet wet, so thick were the logs waiting for the mills at Darien. Sailing ships filled the Darien harbor, waiting to distribute south Georgia's timber to the world.

It was at the spot where an old Indian trail crossed the Altamaha at Fort Barrington that John Bartram first discovered *Franklinia alatamaha*, the plant he named in honor of Benjamin Franklin, his close friend and correspondent. It was near the same place that William Bartram, alone in a canoe, was struck by the beauty of the vast magnolia glades and moved to write one of the finest passages of his book. A bit farther upriver, the tributaries Oconee and Ocmulgee come together at the site of the Indian village of Tama, from which the Altamaha got its name.

On the edge of the swamp, in one of the last cabins of the decaying sawmill village of Doctortown, lives Ambrosia Clark, the last of the Altamaha river rats. Ambrosia remembers when steamboats went up the river to Macon and he can show you the rotting carcass of one not far above town. He remembers the vast schools of shad that spawned in the river. ("They beat their roe out with their tails. It sounded like boards beating the water.") He used to net them and ship them by the barrelful to New York. ("The water was full of them, almost as if you could step across the river on them. There's not but a few now. There's not one channel catfish in ten that was here twenty years ago before the mill came. You can still get three or four shad if you net them. If I was to put a new net in the water this morning I would have to throw it away tomorrow. I guess I ought to make them pay for all the nets that they've ruined.") Asked once what effect the dams presently proposed for the river would have on the shad, Ambrosia said, "That'd wind 'em up."

The Altamaha River Basin Development Commission was established by Governor Maddox and subsidized by funds from the state treasury. (The Commission was de-commissioned by Governor Carter, but is not dead, only dormant.) Two physicians, one from Brunswick and the other from Jesup, are its chiefs. The Commission's motto is "Atlanta to the Atlantic via the Altamaha." The Commission would like to build about twelve dams and locks, one at nearly every shoal and waterfall up to Atlanta and Athens, at a cost of roughly a billion and a half dollars. The Commission held two public hearings at which the plan was praised by commercial and political interests and ardently opposed by the majority of local inhabitants, who are now beginning to organize to protect what is left of their river heritage.

No longer is the Savannah, the river the Creeks called Bluewater, blue. The giant sturgeon are gone from the shoals near the site of Fort Moore, near present-day Augusta, for the waters of the Bluewater are dead, the shoals covered by giant Hartwell dam, built by the Army Corps of Engineers. Now the river flows black to Savannah, fetid with the municipal waste and industrial poisons of Augusta. Its nutrients and sediments are trapped by nine dams, with more proposed. The United States Soil Conservation Service has ditched or plans to ditch many streams in the Savannah basin. Ditching kills a stream and the swampland dependent on it. At Savannah, industrial plants squatting on piles driven far down into the marsh disgorge a hellish potion into the water. The paper mills are particularly gross offenders. Daily the Union-Camp Corporation dumps huge quantities of poison into the river above Savannah, and American Cyanamid discharges 690,000 pounds of acid a day into the river below the city. Savannah itself dumps its untreated sewage into the river.

Of Georgia's three ancient rivers, the Ogeechee alone now flows unimpeded to the sea.

The Satilla, the Yam Gandy, the Little Ocmulgee, the Ohoopee and Canoochee were formed before the freezing of the great Pleistocene ice cap and the consequent lowering of sea level. These lesser rivers assumed strange configurations as they worked their way to the retreating sea. Lacking the power to cut directly through the Pleistocene barrier reefs, they turned and flowed along them until they found a gap or were captured and became tributaries of the three ancient rivers, which had been running for millions of years longer and now had the power to cut through the terraces almost at will. The Satilla runs to the sea unaided, having carved out its own small geological kingdom.

Just after the Civil War, Absolem Chapell wrote in his *Miscellanies of Georgia*, "Here flow the Ohoopies and the Canoochies, the Yam Grandy and the other streams notorious for barren lands, the haunt of deer, and for limped waters rich with fish. Here nature reigns and will continue to reign supreme as she has done for ages past, secure in vast barrens not less mighty than mountains and marshes and deadly climes under equatorial suns, in giving perpetuity to her throne against man's invasions. Here, too, as in other similar pine regions of the South, even war and a dire peace prolific of curses everywhere else, have alike swept over innocuous, inflicting no change. It is grateful to feel that there are some things of earth, not amenable to change at man's hands; some things sacred, stable, ineffaceable in this fickle, fleeting, everperishing world."

Chapell's gratitude was misplaced. Much of the Ohoopee is to be ditched and the Canoochee dammed. Three "stream improvement projects"—channelization schemes—are proposed for Ohoopee tributaries by the United States Soil Conservation Service, and planning is underway. Channelization consists of lowering the drainage of a stream by ditching its central watercourse with draglines. The soil is pushed aside by bulldozers and the surrounding swamplands dry up. Streams are ditched in the name of conservation (though the stream is rendered a biological desert) and in the name of flood control (by draining the swamps that act as sponges during floods, besides filtering out pollution and providing habitat) and in the name of making more cropland available (by the same agency that pays the farmer to take land out of productivity and put it in the soil bank). It is done without any overall plan—all projects are initiated at the local level by committees established by the Soil Conservation Service. Channelization is completed on 36 Georgia streams, underway on 40, and planned for 97 more.

At the old whistle stop at Groveland, where the Seaboard Coast Line crosses the Canoochee, the Groveland Lake Development Authority proposes to build a dam. The state-chartered authority wishes to condemn 20,000 acres of private property, sell 32 million dollars worth of revenue bonds using state credit, build a dam, and sell the surrounding waterfront property to developers for subdivisions and marinas. The only reason given by the promoters for the project is that it will provide the eastern portion of South Georgia with a freshwater lake—there fifty miles from the ocean and in the midst of one of the great wetland topographies in the world.

The Satilla River begins at the confluence of Pudding and Satilla creeks, gathers sustenance from Seventeen Mile, Hurricane, and Sweetwater creeks, and gains its full size after it clears Knickerbocker Swamp. It runs tangent to the north end of Trail Ridge, then turns and flows down the side of that fossil island to the site of Burnt Fort, where Bartram crossed in 1773. Then it heads eastward to the sea. The river has a thousand sinuous curves, each one graced on its "point side" (the inside of the curve; the outside is the "bite side") by a snowy beach imprinted with racoon, deer, turtle, turkey, and sometimes even bear tracks.

In places farther down the Satilla there is now no forest at all for miles, the land having been clear-cut by the pulp mills. All the paper mills clear-cut on their land, taking everything above a foot high and replanting, when they replant at all, with fast-growing pine seedlings that yield a crop in twenty-five to thirty years; then they repeat the same process upon the harvesting of that crop, and thus

are following the practice that devastated the soil of Georgia's Piedmont formation, where the repetitive planting of one crop, cotton, brought about almost total economic collapse.

The Satilla is a naturally fluctuating river. There are times of the year when the Satilla doesn't flow at all, and this has come to concern some men in the town of Waycross. They have formed the Satilla River Improvement Committee, and they plan to "improve" the Satilla by building four water-retention dams on the headwaters of the Pudding, the Seventeen Mile, the Hurricane, and the Sweetwater. They say that when the Satilla is running low they will spill a little water out of those dams. People will be able to build little cabins up there to fish, they say, and, most important, the dams will make the river navigable, so that Waycross can become a port and get some industry.

Dr. Donald C. Scott, for five years the chairman of the Division of Biological Sciences at the University of Georgia, is against damming the Satilla's sources and equalizing the river's year-round flow:

"In most rivers fish reproduction is geared to the seasonal changes in the availability of breeding habitat and food. Some fishes, such as the large-mouthed bass, must breed early in the year; others, such as many species of bream, breed more than once over a longer season. In any case these members of the sunfish family utilize relatively quiet waters for their reproductive activities. The normal occurrence of spring high waters usually provides good conditions for the reproduction of these important game species. The nesting of bass and bream most often occurs in oxbows and the quieter backwaters. The young may mature in these situations and in the river itself. It is obvious that river levels will exert a strong influence on the success or failure of reproduction of many of the inhabitants of the stream, and especially the fish. High water levels expand the habitat, breeding grounds and food supply of fishes. They also increase the total food supply in the river by washing into it organic matter that had accumulated in the swamps and flood plains. When timed right by nature, these conditions can result in the production of a bumper crop of fish. With receding water

It was beginning to be very wild and quiet. I remembered to be frightened and right away I was. It was the beautiful impersonality of the place that struck me the hardest; I would not have believed that it could hit me all at once like this, or with such force. The silence and the silence-sound of the river had nothing to do with any of us.

—JAMES DICKEY

levels, the fish (and other organisms) become concentrated in the river where they are more readily available to man. It is my conclusion that naturally occurring fluctuating water levels are preferable to stabilized flows. Fluctuating levels will produce some years of good fishing and some of bad, while stable flows are likely to result in continuous mediocre fishing. The river will also suffer damage from an esthetic point of view. The beautiful white sand bars for which the river is famous will gradually become covered by vegetation.

"Another aspect of flow stabilization which will create new problems is the effects that this will have on the impoundments constructed to accomplish the stabilization. It is obvious that water will have to be stored when it is plentiful and released when it is in short supply downstream. The impoundments themselves will thus have fluctuating water levels. On the Coastal Plain, where relief is very low, this will mean that large expanses of lake bed will be alternately covered and exposed. This will create conditions which would be unsightly, if not noxious, and will very likely increase the insect problem.

Out of the great swamp that the Indians called *Ouaquaphenogaw*, "Land of the trembling earth"—it was so full of water that its hummocks trembled under their feet— flow two rivers. The river that runs to the south they called *Suwanee*, "River of Reeds." Their name for the river that runs from the swamp first to the south, then east, then north, and finally east again to the sea we do not know, but on the first day of May in 1562, the Frenchman Jean Ribault discovered the river and named it "the River of May." It is now called the St. Mary's.

"After we tarried," wrote Ribault, "we entered and veued the country thereaboute, which is the fairest, frutefullest and pleasantest in all the world with grapes accordingly, which naturally and without man's help and tryming grow to the tops of oaks and other trees that be of wonderful greatness and height and the sight of the faire meadows is a pleasure not able to be expressed with tonge, full of herons, corleau, bitters, mallards, egerles, woodkockes and of all other kinds of small birds, with hartes,

hyndes, buckes, wild swyne and sondery other wilde beastes." The Spanish claimed this to be the pleasantest land in all the world. They drove out the native Timucua, and stayed until 1763, when the English drove *them* out.

The coastal people used to say that of all the Georgia rivers, none was more crooked than the St. Mary's, which flowed for 120 miles where a straight line would run 40; none ran deeper, and none had better drinking water. Sailing vessels would come hundreds of miles off course to obtain water from the St. Mary's for a long voyage, for it was widely known that water contained properties that kept it fresh for months. An old captain once told a local resident that he had preserved St. Mary's water for as long as two years and that at the end of that time it was as good to drink as if it had just been dipped from the river. The water was hauled to Fernandina Harbor and sold to the sailing tramps at the rate of one cent per gallon. St. Mary's water is bright yellow in color, but shows no trace of mud or sediment. The river flows entirely through white-sand country, and the bottom of the river is mostly limestone. The older residents think, and possibly they are right, that the water owes its lasting quality to an acid leached out of palmetto roots and those of other swamp plants, and its sweetness to the limestone.

Today the air above much of the St. Mary's is thick with a pulp-mill odor that in places eats the paint off houses and the chrome off cars. "On a fine, mild November evening," writes Anthony Bailey, "with the wind in the northeast coming over the low green pastures that line Amelia River, you can smell Fernandina from a distance of five miles. You can smell—I should say— Fernandina and St. Mary's . . . Lofty stacks expel tall white plumes of smoke into the air. An eye educated in modern painting might find interest in the complex of whites, slates, grays, and blacks, an industrial, significant (or at any rate striking) form, with light and shadow varying on the smooth and corrugated factory surfaces, and the Coca-Cola-colored water swirling past. But there remains the smell. It is so powerful and acrid that it can't be described, just as you can't describe the taste of food so hot it burns your mouth. Mustard gas must have smelled like that, billowing across the trenches of the Marne."

All the sweet water at the mouth of the St. Mary's is ruined. Since 1941 the Gilman Paper Company has poured its untreated wastes into the river. The owners announced in 1970 that construction would soon start on a $10,000,000 pollution control complex—a fine gesture, but nearly three-quarters of this money is budgeted for a huge recovery boiler designed to aid mill production of more paper for less money, with very little effect on pollution abatement. The manager of the mill has announced that it would be a "very major expenditure" to clean up the North River, an arm of the St. Mary's tidal complex, adding that such a clean-up "will contribute virtually nothing to any segment of the population," and that, "a waste treatment system could not be designed with current knowledge which would surpass the service the North River performs in waste treatment and assimilation . . . these functions are natural and logical stream uses . . . the current and potential value of North River lies solely in waste treatment and limited navigational use."

Before the mill came, the shrimpers and crabbers say, the North River had some of the best fishing on the Atlantic coast. Now they take their boats farther and farther out to sea each year for a dwindling catch. "You take a crab and throw him into the river," one shrimper said recently, pointing at the murky North River beneath his dock. "You know what he'll do? Number one, he'll crawl right out. And number two, he'll die."

The tidal rivers—the Little Ogeechee, the Medway, the North and South Newport, the Sapelo, the Turtle, and the Little Satilla—are an integral part of the marsh, part of a delicate natural system that functions as a single organism, keeping perfect time with the tides. Each of the tidal rivers or one of its important tributaries is scheduled for channelization, or has already been channelized. The Little Ogeechee, the Medway, and the two Newports are scheduled for channelization in the late seventies. Turtle River has already been channelized, but the townspeople say you couldn't hurt it anyway, for the Brunswick Pulp and Paper Company has been dumping waste into the river for so long. The Little Satilla channelization is complete.

The businessmen, the politicians, the Soil Conservation Service, and the Army Corps of Engineers are all pushing toward disaster. The rivers are the arteries of the Georgia coastland, and the fate of the coastland rides on river waters. Dam the rivers and the marshland is dammed; dredge the rivers and the Sea Islands are ruined. The lesson of the coast's recent history should be obvious, yet the improvers persist in their path. The Soil Conservation Service has built up a vast bureaucracy in every county in the state, and has underway the channelization of 174 streams in Georgia alone, 98 of which flow to the coast. The Army Corps of Engineers has built or plans to build 31 major dams on Georgia's eastward-flowing rivers at a cost in excess of three billion dollars. These agencies gain power in proportion to the money they spend. In the destruction of the Georgia coast there is a wealth of power for them, and a near-eternity of poverty for the rest of us. The paper mills of the Georgia coast (with the notable exception of Interstate Paper Company at Riceboro) have discolored the rivers with their effluvia, and filled the air with acrid smoke. They are practicing clearcutting, a one-crop economy of the sort that brought a whole section of our nation to depression less than fifty years ago. The mills draw so much water from underground aquifers that the small farmers of the area are forced to constantly dig deeper wells.

The technology exists to make of the entire Georgia coast a spiritual and biological abattoir. It is up to those of us with nothing to gain from that destruction, and very much to lose, to organize against it.

April, 1973   —ROBERT HANIE

I thought in a panic, I shall never be happy on land again. I was afraid once more of all the painful circumstances of living. But when the dry ground was under us, the world no longer fluid, I found a forgotten loveliness in all the things that have nothing to do with men. Beauty is pervasive, and fills, like perfume, more than the object that contains it. Because I had known intimately a river, the earth pulsed under me.

         —MARJORIE RAWLINGS

Unlike that sudden coming in of the sea to flood the valleys and surge against the mountain crests of the drowned lands of New England, the sea and the land lie here in a relation established gradually, over millions of years.

During those long ages of geologic time, the sea has ebbed and flowed over the great Atlantic coastal plain. It has crept toward the distant Appalachians, paused for a time, then slowly receded, sometimes far into its basin; and on each such advance it has rained down its sediments and left the fossils of its creatures over that vast and level plain. And so the particular place of its stand today is of little moment in the history of the earth or in the nature of the beach—a hundred feet higher, or a hundred feet lower, the seas would still rise and fall unhurried over shining flats of sand, as they do today.

· · ·

Beach, eroding forest, Wassaw Island

The materials of the beach are themselves steeped in antiquity. Sand is a substance that is beautiful, mysterious, and infinitely variable; each grain on a beach is the result of processes that go back into the shadowy beginnings of life, or of the earth itself.

The bulk of seashore sand is derived from the weathering and decay of rocks, transported from their place of origin to the sea by the rains and the rivers. In the unhurried processes of erosion, in the freighting seaward, in the interruptions and resumptions of that journey, the minerals have suffered various fates—some have been dropped, some have worn out and vanished. In the mountains the slow decay and disintegration of the rocks proceed, and the stream of sediments grows—suddenly and dramatically by rockslides—slowly, inexorably, by the wearing of rock by water. All begin their passage toward the sea. Some disappear through the solvent action of water or by grinding attrition in the rapids of a river's bed. Some are dropped on the riverbank by flood waters, there to lie for a hundred, a thousand years, to become locked in the sediments of the plain and wait another million years or so, during which, perhaps, the sea comes in and then returns to its basin. Then at last they are released by the persistent work of erosion's tools—wind, rain, and frost—to resume the journey to the sea. Once brought to salt water, a fresh rearranging, sorting, and transport begin. Light minerals, like flakes of mica, are carried away almost at once; heavy ones like the black sands of ilmenite and rutile are picked up by the violence of storm waves and thrown on the upper beach.

No individual sand grain remains long in any one place. The smaller it is, the more it is subject to long transport—the larger grains by water, the smaller by wind. An average grain of sand is only two and one half times the weight of an equal volume of water, but more than two thousand times as heavy as air, so only the smaller grains are available for transport by wind. But despite the constant working over of the sands by wind and water, a beach shows little visible change from day to day, for as one grain is carried away, another is usually brought to take its place.

. . .

Infinitely small though it is, something of its history may be revealed in the shape and texture of a grain of sand. Wind-transported sands tend to be better rounded than water-borne; furthermore, their surface shows a frosted effect from the abrasion of other grains carried in the blast of air. The same effect is seen on panes of glass near the sea, or on old bottles in the beach flotsam. Ancient sand grains, by their surface etchings, may give a clue to the climate of past ages. In European deposits of Pleistocene sand, the grains have frosted surfaces etched by the great winds blowing off the glaciers of the Ice Age.

We think of rock as a symbol of durability, yet even the hardest rock shatters and wears away when attacked by rain, frost or surf. But a grain of sand is almost indestructible. It is the ultimate product of the work of the waves—the minute, hard core of mineral that remains after years of grinding and polishing. The tiny grains of wet sand lie with little space between them, each holding a film of water about itself by capillary attraction. Because of this cushioning liquid film, there is little further wearing by attrition. Even the blows of heavy surf cannot cause one sand grain to rub against another.

. . .

Bearing on its surface only the wave-carved ripple marks, the fine traceries of sand grains dropped at last by the spent waves, and the scattered shells of long-dead mollusks, the beach has a lifeless look, as though not only uninhabited but indeed uninhabitable. In the sands almost all is hidden. The only clues to the inhabitants of most beaches are found in winding tracks, in slight movements disturbing the upper layers, or in barely protruding tubes and all but concealed openings leading down to hidden burrows.

The signs of living creatures are often visible, if not the animals themselves, in deep gullies that cut the beaches, parallel to the shore line, and hold at least a few inches of water from the fall of one tide until the return of the next. A little moving hill of sand may yield a moon snail intent on predatory errand. A V-shaped track may indicate the presence of a burrowing clam, a sea mouse, a heart urchin. A flat ribbonlike track may lead to a buried sand dollar or a starfish. And wherever protected flats of sand or sandy mud lie exposed between the tides, they are apt to be riddled with hundreds of holes, marked by the sign of the ghost shrimps within. Other flats may bristle with forests of protruding tubes, pencil thin and decorated weirdly with bits of shell or seaweed, an indication that legions of the plumed worm, Diopatra, live below. Or again there may be a wide area marked by the black conical mounds of the lugworm. Or here at the edge of the tide a chain of little parchment capsules, one end free and the other disappearing under the sand, shows that one of the large predatory whelks lies below, busy with the prolonged task of laying and protecting her eggs.

. . .

For most of the fauna of the sand beaches, the key to survival is to burrow into the wet sand, and to possess means of feeding, breathing and reproducing while lying below reach of the surf. And so the story of the sand is in part the story of small lives lived deep within it, finding in its dark, damp coolness a retreat from fish that come hunting with the tide and from birds that forage at the water's edge when the tide has fallen. Once below the surface layers, the burrower has found not only stable conditions but also a refuge where few enemies threaten.

. . .

The shore at night is a different world, in which the very darkness that hides the distractions of daylight brings into sharper focus the elemental realities. Once, exploring the night beach, I surprised a small ghost crab in the searching beam of my torch. He was lying in a pit he had dug just above the surf, as though watching the sea and waiting. The blackness of the night possessed water, air, and beach. It was the darkness of an older world, before Man. There was no sound but the all-enveloping, primeval sound of wind blowing over water and sand, and of waves crashing on the beach. There was no other visible life—just one small crab near the sea.

. . . the same sense of remoteness and of a world apart came to me in a twilight hour on a great beach on the coast of Georgia. I had come down after sunset and walked far out over sands that lay wet and gleaming, to the very edge of the retreating sea. Looking back across that immense flat, crossed by winding, water-filled gullies and here and there holding shallow pools left by the tide, I was filled with awareness that this intertidal area, although abandoned briefly and rhythmically by the sea, is always reclaimed by the rising tide. There at the edge of low water the beach with its reminders of the land seemed far away. The only sounds were those of the wind moving over water, and another of water sliding over the sand and tumbling down the faces of its own wave forms. The flats were astir with birds, and the voice of the willet rang insistently. . . .

The flat took on a mysterious quality as dusk approached and the last evening light was reflected from the scattered pools and creeks. Then birds became only dark shadows, with no color discernible. Sanderlings scurried across the beach like little ghosts, and here and there the darker forms of the willets stood out. Often I could come very close to them before they would start up in alarm—the sanderlings running, the willets flying up, crying. Black skimmers flew along the ocean's edge silhouetted against the dull, metallic gleam.

. . .

On all these shores there are echoes of past and future: of the flow of time, obliterating yet containing all that has gone before; of the sea's eternal rhythms—the tides, the beat of surf, the pressing rivers of the currents— shaping, changing, dominating; of the stream of life, flowing as inexorably as any ocean current, from past to unknown future. For as the shore configuration changes in the flow of time, the pattern of life changes, never static, never quite the same from year to year. Whenever the sea builds a new coast, waves of living creatures surge against it, seeking a foothold, establishing their colonies. And so we come to perceive life as a force as tangible as any of the physical realities of the sea, a force strong and purposeful, as incapable of being crushed or diverted from its ends as the rising tide.

—Rachel Carson

1. Old Beaches, New Beaches

The Georgia shoreline was once two hundred miles inland of its present mark. At Columbus and Macon and Augusta you can still see vestiges of that ancestral shore, sand dunes 136,000,000 years old. An ancient ocean abandoned the dunes and retreated toward the rising sun, exposing new land as it went. The land that would later be called *Guale* by its first human inhabitants rose from the sea. From the Cretaceous through the Tertiary the ocean withdrew in seven distinct stages, at the end of which the Georgia shoreline stood one hundred miles farther out to sea than it does now. The ocean rose for a time, and then in the Pleistocene again retreated seven times.

The life of Georgia's vast new coastal plain varied greatly with the cold of glacial advance and the warmth of glacial retreat. In cold periods spruce forests grew as far south as Louisiana, and walrus hunted the waters off the Georgia coast. In the hot periods the plain was something like the present savanna of Africa. Shaggy, four-tusked mastodons wandered there, and true elephants larger than any of Africa's. There were lions, saber-toothed cats, cougars, bobcats, rhinoceroses, giant armadillo-like glyptodons, beavers as big as bears, camels, llamas, tapirs, peccaries, deer, dire wolves, horses, and several species of bison. There was megatherium, a ground sloth eighteen feet long. Its bones were massive—the femur was three times as thick as an elephant's—and the sloth must have weighed several tons. It was a slow-moving vegetarian of enormous strength. There was entelodont, a gigantic, nearly brainless pig that stood six feet at the shoulder. Great companies of these creatures wandered between the edge of the sea and the inland forests of magnolia, tupelo, sweetgum, tulip poplar, cypress, and other subtropical trees.

The ancient shorelines of Georgia, like the present one, were protected by chains of barrier islands. There is no consensus on how such barrier islands are formed. One theory, proposed by de Beaumont in 1845, is that the islands began as offshore sandbars. The bars themselves were formed then as they are now, when waves traveling across shallow water become steep, break, lose energy, and dump their loads of sand. The sand of millions of waves becomes a bar, the bar rises in time above the water, dunes develop, and finally an island forms. In 1967 John Hoyt,

then Acting Director of the University of Georgia Marine Institute, proposed a new theory. Unable to find, in drilling on the mainland shores nearest Georgia's barrier islands, any evidence of the old marine beach that de Beaumont's theory would seem to require, Hoyt suggested that submergence was the answer. Waves and wind formed dunes along the ancient beaches, according to Hoyt's new scheme. The dunes grew and stabilized. There were periods of minor submergence, but if the dunes were large and stable enough they were not washed away. They became barrier islands, with the shallow invading waters forming lagoons on the landward sides and the ocean proper beating ·on their seaward beaches. In time the lagoons filled with riverine sediment and became salt marshes. With each of the seven Pleistocene retreats of the sea, as the cold of the ice age deepened and the polar ice caps grew, tying up more of the ocean's waters, another barrier-island shoreline was left high and dry.

With each eastward retreat of the sea from the continent, the land was revealed in successively lower terraces. Raw rivulets and primitive springs on the new terrain were worked upon by sun, wind, rain, frost, and life, and soon rivers threaded the new landscape. With each retreat, the rivers cut more deeply into the terraces, carrying away the sediments that would enrich the coastal marshland, working their way past relict shorelines in pursuit of the receding sea.

The traveler who canoes today down any of the coastal rivers of Georgia dips his paddle into black waters, and watches a green forest unfolding on either side as the river serpentines seaward; he glimpses, perhaps, the red-white-black flash of a pileated woodpecker; he passes through cypress swamps, the gnarled and bulbous cypress trunks in regiments all around him, and stops and spends the night on a half-moon sand bar. He continues on in the morning, the inland air now full of featherlike willow seeds and dragonflies, and rounds a curve to see, right where it shouldn't be, a golden wall of sand forty feet high, a dune in the forest, as incongruous as a stranded whale here seventy miles from the sea.

If the traveler starts far enough inland, he is confronted five times by landlocked Pleistocene islands. (The local people call them bluffs or ridges.) Inevitably the rivers

turn when they reach the inland side of each fossil archipelago. They usually flow southward down the backside until they find an opening and can flow again toward the sea. Five times the traveler floats through cypress swamp that was once salt marshland behind a coastal island. Okeefenokee, the greatest swamp of all, was once marshland behind the greatest barrier island of all, Trail Ridge, which is a part of the oldest and westernmost of Pleistocene shorelines. Remnants of that shoreline, the first of the five that the river traveler encounters, are collectively called "Wicomico," and were formed perhaps a half million years ago in the Yarmouth Interglacial Period, which left the sea one hundred feet higher than it is now.

A few miles east of the Wicomico bluff, the traveler floats into, and eventually around, the remnants of the second barrier-island shoreline, the Penholoway, formed when the sea was 75 feet higher than it is presently. Then the Talbot shoreline, formed when the sea was 45 feet higher, then the Pamlico, 25 feet higher, then the Princess Ann, 15 feet.

The present shoreline, with its half million acres of marsh and nine major barrier islands, was formed in the last two stages of the Ice Age and is made up of two barrier systems. The first, the Silver Bluff shoreline, was created by a sea five feet higher and 40,000 years older than the Atlantic we know, and the second, the Holocene shoreline, is presently being formed by today's waves. Each nascent Holocene island has a shadow island of Silver Bluff age, older than and westward of it, and from which it has taken over duties as barrier to the sea. In some places the Holocene island and its shadow have merged. Ossabaw, St. Catherines, Sapelo, St. Simons, Jekyll, and Cumberland have both a Holocene half and a Silver Bluff half. Tybee island is separate from its counterpart Wilmington, however, and Wassaw is separate from Skidaway. The Holocene islands have a poorly developed soil, for they are very new and there has been little time for soil to form. The Silver Bluff islands have a mature soil profile, with humus from three to eight feet deep.

The life of the present beach gives a fair idea of what life was like on the five Pleistocene coastlines from which it has descended, as well as of the life on the seven Cretaceous and Tertiary coastlines behind them. The paperthin horsehoe crab, essentially unchanged for 350 million years and not really a crab at all—its nearest kin are the spider and scorpion—still lives here. There is the tiny slipper limpet, its shell shaped like a silver moccasin, and the orange-lined whelk, shaped like a hand rattle, that the *Guale*, as the coastal Indians named themselves, used for a dipper. There is the hard-shelled clam that the Indians call *quahog*. Great piles of quahog shells can be seen all up and down the coast at Guale campsites, along with heaps from other members of ancient shellfish families: the eastern oyster, the Atlantic ribbed mussel, the Atlantic razor clam, the knobbed whelk, the channeled whelk, and the yellow marsh periwinkle. The beach is home for starfish, sea cucumbers, sea urchins, sand dollars, sea lilies, burgundy-colored sea pansies, magenta sea fans, and pink calico, fiddler, and ghost crabs.

Of the ghost crab, Rachel Carson writes, "The individual crab in its brief life epitomizes the protracted racial drama, the evolutionary coming-to-land of a sea creature. The larva, like that of the mole crab, is oceanic, becoming a creature of the plankton once it has hatched from the egg that has been incubated and aerated by the mother. As the infant crab drifts in the currents it sheds its cuticle several times to accommodate the increasing size of its body; at each molt it undergoes slight changes of form. Finally the last larval stage, called the megalops, is reached. This is the form in which all the destiny of the race is symbolized, for it—a tiny creature alone in the sea—must obey whatever instinct drives it shoreward, and must make a successful landing on the beach. The long processes of evolution have fitted it to cope with its fate. Its structure is extraordinary when compared with like stages of closely related crabs. Jocelyn Crane, studying these larvae in various species of ghost crabs, found that the cuticle is always thick and heavy, the body rounded. The appendages are grooved and sculptured so that they may be folded down tightly against the body, each fitting precisely against the adjacent ones. In the hazardous act of coming ashore, these structural adaptations protect the young crab against the battering of the surf and the scraping of sand."

On certain summer moonlit nights on the beaches of Ossabaw, Sapelo, and Cumberland, huge, barnacle-encrusted, female loggerhead and green turtles—"heavy as chests of plate, with vast shells medallioned and orbed like shields . . . newly crawled forth from beneath the foundations of the world," as Herman Melville wrote—emerge from the black ocean and scrape in over the sand. They scoop out nests in the sand with their back legs, lay as many as a hundred white eggs the size of ping-pong balls, cover the nests, and drag themselves back into the sea.

Even the birdlife of this coast is ancient. The shorebirds: loons, grebes, petrels, pelicans, cormorants, anhingas, herons, egrets, bitterns, plovers, and curlews, are the most primitive of avians. Not only do they resemble reptiles in flight—the snake-necked water turkey, for example, as it feeds and flies in the marsh—but they also contain much kindred bone structure. Peter Matthiessen,

in *Shorebirds of North America*, writes that, "*Charadrius*, the genus which includes the piping plover, the *Numenius*, the genus of the modern curlews, are found in the fossil records of 65 million years ago, and to this day the piping plover retains the body scales, condyle bone sockets, air sacs, nuculated red corpuscles, eggs and egg teeth in the young, which are the heritage of the reptilian ancestor."

The present Georgia shoreline is very new, but it tells an old story.

Simple, salt-water-resistant plants live on the island beaches down near the water. These hardy evergreens are the first to come to new-formed dunes, their seeds borne there by birds, wind, and waves. Not very far back from where the tides have strewn edible green sea lettuce, dulse, and Irish moss in a thousand careless arcs, grow sea rocket, hogwort, and pennywort, their roots anchored in the drier sand, all edible themselves and overshadowed by sea oats and sand spurs. Inland of these is the yucca, with the sword-shaped leaves that earned it the name "Spanish bayonet." In the spring the yucca produces clusters of globular white flowers. Growing in the same zone is the prickly pear, whose thorns protect a reddish-green fruit, a favorite food of the islands' many raccoons. Around copses of seaside goldenrod, panic grass grows in wavy fields, turning crimson in the fall. Sweet-smelling red cedars, or junipers, hung with clusters of cerulian balls, grow in the sandy soil, along with the scarlet-berried yaupon or cassina bush, the leaves of which the Guale dried to brew their holy drink. The tropical cabbage palm grows behind the beach, its heart edible and formerly boiled by the Indians in bear fat for porridge. Growing near it is the fanlike saw palmetto, the fronds of which the Indians used for mats, baskets, and roofs. Scrawny wax myrtles, from whose berries the white man made sweet bayberry candles, range widely, as do live oaks. Standing behind the dunes, the oaks are shaped by the wind into a continuous canopy that echoes the dune's form. Within the canopy, the leafless lower limbs of the oaks are clothed with molds and lichen.

As the islands widened with the formation of new dunes, the plant communities extended themselves. With age and the accretion of sediment and organic matter, the older parts of the island grew forests predominated by the live oaks. The oaks sometimes yield a bit of ground to *Magnolia grandiflora* (called *Tolo-chlucco*, "the big bay," by

the Indians) and to the red bay (*Eto-mico*, "the king's tree") and to hickory, laurel oak, holly, and hawthorn. In those places where the ancient oaks have been destroyed by fire or the works of man (*Old Ironsides* and other frigates of her period were made of Sea-island oak) there are expanses of dwarfed and twisted dogwood trees. Spanish moss hangs from nearly every live oak limb on the islands, tinctured a greenish-yellow by the rains and sharing its niche often with a desiccated brown plant that the rains transform into the dainty, mint-green resurrection fern. The same rains bring new sustenance to the green mold and velvet moss, and give new color to the strawberry lichen. The live oak limbs sometimes stretch one hundred feet outward from the trunk, often resting on the ground like elbows before turning upward again toward the sun. Their joints are chocked with orange bracket fungus, and their arms entwined by miles of thick wild-grape vines, which in turn are intertwined by the vines of sparkleberry, sweetleaf, Virginia creeper, crossvine, and the vine whose flower appears in January, the tiny, lemon-yellow, trumpet-shaped, sweet-smelling jasmine. The most colorful bird in North America, the painted bunting, makes its spring and summer home in this tangle. The Georgia coast is one of the few places in the Northern Hemisphere graced with fragrant flowers and singing birds in January.

In the oldest forests of the islands, where clusters of the *Magnolia grandiflora* are found among the oaks, the air is sweet throughout the year. The *grandiflora's* tulip-shaped flower when its white petals are peeled back, reveals a cadmium heart. The flower, though larger than two hands held together, gives off the faintest perfume. The smell mingles nicely with the odor of the tiny, white-flowered osmanthus, and is overwhelmed in places by the noxious-

sweet aroma of palmetto and palm flowers. The musky stillness of the forest is broken only by gentle tremors in the evergreen leaves.

Ancient dunes run along the islands like parallel railroad tracks. The slivers of salt marsh that once lay between these dunes were filled long ago, and freshwater sloughs, lakes, and ponds lie there now. Some are fed by rainwater, others by artesian springs. This is the "blackwater" where leaves, moss, and vines have fallen into the still water and given up their lignins and tannins to it, producing a black liquor. In January the willows, gums, cypresses, and cottonwoods of the lakes and sloughs stand leafless, and the water itself is barren, except sometimes for the spinning wisps of the tiny green aquatic plant called "duckweed." In March come cattail spears, arrowhead, water lilies, purple pickerel weed, and the tiny white bladderwort. By April the larger sloughs all up and down the coast are filled with thousands of birds: snowy, cattle, and common egrets on Ossabaw Island; Louisiana, little blue, and great blue herons on Sapelo; black skimmers on Little St. Simons Island; and all these *and* the white and glossy ibises on Cumberland.

By October the last of the birds have gone from the rookeries, and the sloughs are silent once more. Occasional mallards and teal (or greenwings, as they are commonly called on the islands) pass through. The leaves overhead have already begun to turn their autumnal reds and yellows. The cypress hangs out the slough's most stunning sign of fall as each of its needles turns a flaming orange, an orange more orange than the cantherallus mushroom that stands all over the islands after fall rains, more orange even than the lining of the knobbed whelk down on the beach.

2. The Marsh

The tides make Sapelo an island. First it is set off by water on all sides, open ocean to the east, and marsh with just the tips of grass showing to the west; then six hours later it seems a part of the mainland, a bit of forest separated from the coastal plain forests by a broad grassy savannah.

—MILDRED and JOHN TEAL

As many as five miles of marshland separate the islands from the sea. The marshes are supplied from one direction by nutrients and sediment brought down by the fourteen rivers, and from the other by the very high tides of this coast. In 1663 William Hilton described the result: "The country abounds with grapes, large figs, and peaches; the woods with deer, conies, turkeys, quails, curlues, plovers, teile, herons; and as the Indians say, in winter with swans, geese, cranes, ducks and mallard, and innumberable of other water fowls, whose names we know not, which lie in the rivers, marshes, and on the sands: oysters of abundance, with great store of muscles; a sort of fair crabs, and a round shell fish called horse feet; the rivers stored plentifully with fish we saw play and leap."

The cordgrasses, genus Spartina, are the dominant plants of the marshes. *Spartina alterniflora* grows tall beside the tidal creeks, and thinner and shorter inland on the marsh plains, where it is joined by more of the grass family; needle rushes or juncus, saltgrass, glasswort, salt-meadow cordgrass, panic grass, and then, nearest dry land, sea oxye, cattails, sea lavender, wild rice, seaside golden-rod, and marsh elder. The tidal marsh soil is the most fertile and productive on earth. It contains more organisms per square foot than any soil on earth, and out on those vast glades myriad birds, mammals, and crustaceans come for the marine microörganisms, salts, and nutrients left by incoming tides. Outgoing tides carry the largess of the marsh out to sea, where it feeds still more creatures.

All days are open over the salt marsh. Like a treeless plain, it is a place for the sky to enter. Its wide, seaward stretches with fiddler crabs, ribbed mussels, and snails, with gulls stalking, pools flicking with saltwater minnows, creeks with fingerling fish, are tidally oriented, ground that is neither beach nor dry land, but something in between—a moist region forever in wait for the next return or withdrawal of the sea. It is a refuge for migrants of the air, the ducks and geese. Rains slant over it unobstructed. Winter winds sweep stiffly across it. The sunset fires go out over long horizons. Light shafts penetrate enormous clouds overhead. And in the early autumn the winds blow full and loose over land and sea.

—JOHN HAY and PETER FARB

The fact is, that the two elements are so fused hereabouts that there are hardly such things as earth or water proper; that which styles itself the former is a fat, muddy, slimy sponge, that, floating half under the turbid river, looks yet saturated with the thick waves which every now and then reclaim their late dominion, and cover it almost entirely; the water, again, cloudy and yellow, like pea-soup, seems but a solution of such islands, rolling turbid and thick with alluvium, which it both gathers and deposits as it sweeps along with a swollen, smooth rapidity, that almost deceives the eye. . . . But then the sky— . . . the saffron brightness of the morning, the blue intense brilliance of noon, the golden splendor and the rosy softness of sunset.

—Frances Kemble

The wetlands are filled with smells. They smell of the sea and salt water and of the edge of the sea, the sea with a little iodine and a trace of dead life. The marshes smell of Spartina, a fairly strong odor mixed from the elements of sea and the smells of grasses. These are clean, fresh smells, smells that are pleasing to one who lives by the sea but strange and not altogether pleasing to one who has always lived inland.

—JOHN and MILDRED TEAL

At low tide, the wind blowing across Spartina grass sounds like wind on the
prairie. When the tide is in, the gentle music of moving water is added
to the prairie rustle. There are sounds of birds living in the marshes.
The marsh wren advertises his presence with a reedy call, even at night, when
most birds are still. The marsh hen, or clapper rail, calls in a loud, carrying
cackle. You can hear the tiny, high-pitched rustling thunder of the herds
of crabs moving through the grass as they flee before advancing feet or
the more leisurely sound of movement they make on their daily migrations
in search of food. At night, when the air is still and other sounds are quieted,
an attentive listener can hear the bubbling of air from the sandy soil
as a high tide floods the marsh.

—JOHN and MILDRED TEAL

Marsh, Tybee Island

Marsh grass, Cumberland

The great character of marshes lies in their wide and various use of the
elements that invest them. They contain grasses whose roots are wet with salt
water all the time; grasses and plants that are accustomed to occasional
wetting or alternate flooding by the tides; grasses, sedges, and reeds that
are adapted to being exposed to the sun, strong winds, and salt spray.
If a salt marsh merges with a brackish and then a freshwater environment, the
transitional zone may be wide and gradual enough to contain any number of
life forms.

—JOHN HAY and PETER FARB

A marsh is so rich in life, it involves so many intricate relationships, it nourishes the young of so many different species under so many different conditions of area and relative salinity, that adequate studies of it are only just beginning. It stands between land and sea, taking from both and giving to both, comprising a network of complex ecological strings that tie the unity of the ocean's edge together. The marsh acts as a great sponge, absorbing tremendous amounts of moisture, and as a protective buffer for the land against storm waves and flood tides.

In order to convince one another on its behalf, we keep reiterating the facts about a marsh's organic matter, its production in terms of so many tons an acre, a production as rich or richer than farm land in Iowa, its value as a spawning area for game fish such as striped bass and flounder, or for the shrimp that abound in its brackish estuaries. The tidal marsh, the tidal creek or estuary, the wide, flat, springy ground covered with tough grasses, the peat that is its foundation, are thus of measurable economic importance. At the same time, it may be said that we can live without shrimp, sea bass, flounder, or shellfish, those of us, at least, who are not directly involved with that kind of livelihood, and most of us are not. To argue that the destruction of salt marshes results in a tremendous loss of productive energy that may have serious effects on our economy is like repeating the statistics about how the number of trees and birds has decreased and how much topsoil has been lost. Four hundred thousand acres blow or wash away every year, but not necessarily my half acre or city. . . .

Perhaps it is as an open and at the same time untouched and secret place, a matrix of variety, complex and wild, full of the new and renewing colors, changes and motions that we admire in all nature, that we have to defend a salt marsh, a place we can still go to to learn, to be enlightened.

—JOHN HAY and PETER FARB

3. Jessie Bailey

There is a fitness in natural experience, an intimacy, that may not be superseded.
How many, in this world of devices, now live through a lifetime of tides, nights of clean
wind and clear stars above the roofline, know genuine exposure to cold rain, cold water
and stiff fingers, know how to be steady there?

—JOHN HAY

Jessie Bailey's dirty white dog Brad is far more congenial on land than Jessie is. Brad is so congenial in fact that he is a nuisance, but Jessie, on land, is almost a ghost. Jessie lives on Cumberland Island, on the bluff called High Point, where he works for the Candler family. He is a man of no foolishness and yes or no answers. Occasionally after supper Jessie comes down to the old hotel that is now the Candler home, and if Candler's Yellowstone Bourbon touches him just right that night, he begins talking his haunting Gullah, but since no one else on the island understands that tongue, it does not make for conversation. Jessie's real life is not lived in the society of men. His true home is not on land, but down in the salt marsh of Christmas Creek. Jessie was born on Sapelo Island, where his people have lived since slavery days, but Christmas Creek on Cumberland is his adopted country.

A vast expanse of tidal marsh separates Big Cumberland from Little Cumberland Island. Christmas Creek drains all that marsh through a number of serpentine channels.

The creek is named Christmas because it is full of gifts; its marsh is a nursery for the sea, and life, preying and preyed upon, eating and edible, is as abundant in its dendritic maze of tributaries as anywhere on earth.

Jessie goes down to Christmas Creek when the tide is low and the murky, life-laden waters are running out. He descends the dock's five barnacled steps to his gray bateau and wordlessly arranges his nets and buckets. The marsh grass is still dripping on either side and the water smells like natural chowder. He pushes the charcoal firepot he uses for night fishing out of his way and gives his passenger, when he brings one, a croker sack to sit on, directing him to the middle of the boat. If the kicker won't start he curses violently and agglutinatively, running all the swear words together. The motor finally starts and Jessie turns the prow of his bateau downstream, running seaward with the falling ten-foot ebb tide. He lights a Camel and holds it between tobacco-stained fingers. He smokes and looks about him.

The [Cumberland] salt marsh is the most extensive one south of the Chesapeake. It is dominated by cord grass that rises higher than a man's head. The higher the tide, the higher the grass in a tidal marsh, and the Georgia coast has seven-foot tides. An acre of that marsh is ten times as fertile as the most fertile acre in Iowa. Roots of the cord grass reach down into the ooze and mine nutrients. When the grass dies and crumbles, it becomes high-protein detritus. Shrimp spend a part of their life cycle in there eating the crumbled grass. In the marsh, too, is a soup of microscopic plants, of phosphorus, nitrogen, calcium. Oysters grow there. Fish feed in the marshes and on marsh foods washed by the tides. If a quarter acre of marsh could be lifted up and shaken in the air, anchovies would fall out, and crabs, menhaden, croakers, butterfish, flounders, tonguefish, squid. Bigger things eat the things that eat the marsh, and thus the marsh is the broad base of a marine-food pyramid that ultimately breaks the surface to feed the appetite of man.

Tidal creeks penetrate Cumberland Island, and along their edges, when the tide is low, hundreds of thousands of oysters are exposed to view. Shrimp, fast-wiggling and translucent, feed between the beds of oysters. No wonder the Indians wanted to be buried on Cumberland Island.

—JOHN McPHEE

Jessie's marsh clothes—worn denim jacket, gray khaki pants stuffed into gum boots, a crofter's hat—are all becoming. The clothes are smeared with mud and with each trip are becoming more and more a part of the marsh, and of Jessie.

Jessie turns left in a slow, wide arc up a smaller tidal creek. The banks begin to close up very fast on either side. He enters a tidal pool ringed by oyster beds and he cuts the motor. The bateau comes to a smoking, fluttering stop. Jessie poles the boat over to the nearest oyster bed and pokes at the oysters like a man stirring up a fire. He picks some and throws them in the boat, pitching the rejected oysters back onto the bed. The chunks of selected oysters make a screeching sound against the bottom.

When he has collected enough from this bed, Jessie rolls his sleeves above the elbows and gets down on his knees facing the prow, as if to make a blessing. He plunges his arm over the side and searches the silt-laden bottom, pulls up black clams, and bangs them on the floor of the boat. He talks to the clams, giving them feminine names and cajoling them. He counts them by twos, and when he is satisfied that he has enough from this spot, he returns to his feet and poles downstream to another. This time he steps out on the marsh bank to get just the medium-sized oysters he wants. The bottom of the boat disappears under oysters. When he decides he has enough for the two big croker sacks awaiting him back at the dock, he bends once more to grope for clams. Like a blind man he gathers them by touch until he has an even dozen.

Tidal creek, Cumberland

Oysters on the half shell, when they are as fresh as the ones we ate for lunch that day, are so shining and translucent, to nearly transparent, that if you were to drop one on a printed page you could read words through the oyster. I had lived beside tidal creeks at various times in the past, and had once set up my own amateur oyster farm, from which I regularly removed a hundred and forty-four oysters each day to eat before lunch, but even the memory of my oyster farm was turned slightly opaque by the quality of the oysters from Candler's tidal creek. Mantle to palpi, each vitrescent blob was a textural wonder. We ate at least five hundred of them, raw or roasted (over an oak fire)–*Ostrea virginica,* better than the best oysters of Bordeaux.

—JOHN McPHEE

Jessie starts the motor and runs farther upstream, to a place where the falling tide has left smaller pools behind oyster dams. He takes out his catch net, stands in the prow, pulls the slip noose over his right wrist, places the "bullet" of one of the net's lead weights in his mouth, spreads the net with his left arm, and flings it out into the pool, following through with his whole body. The sixty bullets take the net down instantly. Jessie draws it slowly in and dumps its catch of flopping mullet and white-bellied sea trout on the bottom of the bateau. He continues to cast. Sometimes the net comes back empty, and sometimes with several fish, and sometimes with many. The bateau seems to make slow progress upstream with this easy casting and drawing in. At last he pushes the fish into a pile with his foot, starts his motor, and heads down just in time to beat the tide over the oyster dams.

Back in the main channel, Jessie continues downstream a short distance, then cuts the motor and lets the boat drift down next to the bank. Reaching over the side he searches with his fingers and comes up with conchs; white spiral shells and large muscular feet. He tosses them on the floor. The boat is now full of food and the tide has ebbed, so Jessie returns to the dock.

Later in the evening, Jessie prepares his sea feast. He cooks beneath a grove of live oaks near the High Point Hotel, built around 1870 and covered with Moorish white gingerbread. He shovels the wild supper onto a sheet of corrugated tin braced over a smoking, heart-pine fire. The oilcloth covered table is garnished with onions, carrots, and lettuce from Jessie's garden. A big bowl of wild salad—sea rocket, cattails, pennywort and wild mint, gathered that afternoon from Cumberland's dunes, marshes, and woods—sits at one end, and near it is a soufflé made of fresh squash, bacon, cracker crumbs, and butter. Each guest's place is marked by a napkin, an awl, and a can of beer. At the center of the table is a large box of saltines and a communal bowl of sauce, mixed of catsup, horseradish, worcestershire, and lemon juice. The clams come first as hors d'oeuvres. Jessie serves the rest with a pitchfork. Each guest offers the choicest of his oysters to his neighbor—the best custom at a High Point oyster roast—and through it all Jessie says not a word.

Cumberland Island, a third larger than Manhattan, has a population of eleven. Its beach is a couple of hundred yards wide and consists of a white sand that is fine and soft to the touch. The beach is just under twenty miles long, and thus, although there are no obstructions whatever, it is impossible to see from one end of it to the other, because the beach itself drops from sight with the curve of the earth. Wild horses, gray and brown, roam the beach, apparently for the sheer pleasure of the salt air. Poachers round them up from time to time and sell them to rodeos for fifteen dollars apiece. Wild pigs seem to like the Cumberland beach, too. The figure of a man is an unusual thing there.

. . .

New, young dunes rise behind the beach, and behind the dunes are marshes, fresh or tidal. In some of the marshes and in ponds and lakes elsewhere on the island live alligators fourteen feet long. The people of the island will not say specifically where the alligators are. They are fond of their tremendous reptiles. Poachers, commando-fashion, come for them by night, kill them, and take just the hides. Behind the marshes stand the old dunes, high, smooth as talc, sloped precipitously like lines of cresting waves, and covered with pioneer grasses. At the back of the dunes begins a live-oak forest. The canopies of the oaks nearest the beach have been so pruned by the wind that they appear to have been shaped by design in a medieval garden. Among the oaks are slash pines and red cedars—trees also tolerant of salt. Sand-lane roads wind through the forest. Poachers use them in pursuit of white-tailed deer. Hotels in Jacksonville pay thirty-five dollars a deer. Through the woods run thousands of wild pigs. Now and again, a piglet is stopped by a diamondback.

A generally high bluff rims the western shore of the island, and along it are irregular humps—Indian burial mounds that have never been opened. Watched from the bluff, sunsets gradually spread out over a salt marsh five miles wide. This distance from the mainland in part explains why Cumberland Island remains as it is at this apparently late date in the history of the world. There is no bridge.

. . .

We drove up a marching dune and snowplowed down the other side, leaving fresh tracks in the powdery white sand. The wind would cover them. But how many tracks could the wind cover? Since early morning—in fact, for three days—we had roamed an island bigger than Manhattan and had seen no one on its beach and, except at Candler's place and Greyfield, no one in its interior woodlands. In the late twentieth century, in this part of the world, such an experience was unbelievable. The island was a beautiful and fragile anachronism. We were, as Candler had said, seeing what the Indians saw, and it was not at all difficult to understand why he wanted to "live where the Indians lived . . . closer to the earth, a part of the environment." We, too, had eaten from the tidal creeks and had gone where and how we pleased—a privilege made possible in our time by private ownership. That was the irony of Cumberland Island and the index of its fate. The island was worth nothing when the Muskhogean Creeks lived and fished there. Now it was worth at least ten million dollars, a figure that could swell beyond recognition. Need, temptation, and realistic taxes would eventually wrest the island from its present owners. They would not be able to afford it. The question whether it was right for a few individuals to own twenty miles of beach had already been bypassed by these inexorable facts of economics. . . .

In the battle for Cumberland Island, there could be human winners here or there, but—no matter what might happen—there could be no victory for Cumberland Island. The Frasers of the world might create their blended landscapes, the Park Service its Yosemites. Either way, or both ways, no one was ever to be as free on that wild beach in the future as we had been that day.

—JOHN McPHEE

4. First Men

The first human inhabitants came down to the marshes much as Jessie Bailey does today. The Guale moved through the marsh grasses and island oaks and bays, synchronous with the movements of the tides and seasons, and they called themselves and the land by the same name.

Above the Guale lived the Cusabo and below them the Timucua, all members of the Muskhogean or Creek Confederacy, which comprised fifty-six tribes and stretched across a great part of what is now the Southeastern United States. William Bartram, an early visitor of these tribes, described them:

"The males of the Cherokees, Muscogulges, Siminoles, Chicasaws, Chactaws and confederate tribes of the Creeks, are tall, erect, and moderately robust, their limbs well shaped, so as generally to form a perfect human figure; their features regular, and countenance open, dignified and placid; yet the forehead and brow so formed, as to strike you instantly with heroism and bravery; the eye though rather small, yet active and full of fire; the pupil always black, and the nose commonly inclining to the aquiline.

"Their countenance and actions exhibit an air of magnanimity, superiority and independence.

"Their complexion of a reddish brown or copper colour; their hair long, lank, coarse and black as a raven, and reflecting the like lustre at different exposures to the light.

"The women of the Cherokees are tall, slender, erect and of a delicate frame, their features formed with perfect symmetry, their countenance cheerful and friendly, and they move with a becoming grace and dignity.

"The Muscogulge women, though remarkably short of stature, are well formed; their visage round, features regular and beautiful; the brow high and arched; the eye large, black and languishing, expressive of modesty, diffidence, and bashfulness; these charms are their defensive and offensive weapons, and they know very well how to play them off. And under cover of these alluring graces, are concealed the most subtile artifice; they are however loving and affectionate."

The Guale lived in forty villages up and down the islands. The paramount chief lived at the Guale capital on the island of Guale, now called St. Catherines. North of Guale Island were villages on the islands called Ossapo, Wassaw, and Tybee. South of Guale were villages on Asao, Osoa, and Missoe, now called St. Simons, Jekyll, and Cumberland, and on Sapala, now called Sapelo.

We know little about the Guale, for their customs did not withstand white men long enough to be recorded. They were a race of robust men and tall and agile women. Both sexes wore their jet-black hair long. They decorated their bodies with tattoos and painted their faces with brilliant colors. They daubed themselves with bear fat as protection from the sun and kept their fingernails long for eating and fighting. They wore very little clothing except for the deerskin loincloths worn by the men and the skirts woven of moss for the women. Gorgets, necklaces, and anklets of shell were worn by both men and women. Their round homes, usually small and containing few possessions, were made of a frame of pine limbs covered with the bark of gum, cypress, and cedar, and floored with woven cane mats that often had a scarlet fringe. Their hunting and gathering diet of fish and fowl, roots, herbs, and flowers was supplemented at some point in their sojourn on the coast by maize, peas, pumpkins, squash, and melons, the seeds of which are thought to have arrived from civilizations farther south.

In 1539 De Soto marched from his landing in Florida across Georgia to the Savannah River, making a sport of killing the Indian men and raping the Indian women, and enslaving them both as beasts of burden. The Portuguese "Gentleman of Elvas," who was most probably Alvaro Fernandez, in his *Narrative of the Expedition of Hernando Desoto* describes the method: "Two captains having been sent in opposite directions, in quest of Indians, a hundred men and women were chosen out for the governor as was always customary for the officers to do after successful inroads, dividing the others among themselves and companions. They were led off in chains, with collars about their necks, to carry luggage and grind corn, doing the labor proper to servants." The same writer records the arrival of the expedition at the town of Achese on the Ocmulgee River, and sets down his version of the speech of the town's chief:

"Very high, powerful and good master: The things that seldom happen bring astonishment. Think, then, what must be the effect on me and mine, of the sight of you and your people, whom we have at no time seen, astride the fierce brutes, your horses, entering with such

The Franciscans had probably many hardships to bear, but there were compensations. The climate of the islands was delightful, mild in winter and moderated in summer by cool breezes from the ocean, and it was a place of abundance. The native fishermen caught shrimps, crabs, and turtles, as well as a great variety of fish, and the hunters shot wild turkeys and deer, which they brought over to the islands and sold for a trifling sum. Figs, oranges, and pomegranates were planted and flourished, and the good Fathers must have felt that this land, contrasted with the cold and aridity of most of Spain, was an earthly Paradise.

—CAROLINE LOVELL

speed and fury into my country, that we had no tidings of your coming—things so altogether new, as to strike terror to our hearts."

De Soto told the chief that he was a child of the sun and that he came seeking gold. Then he erected a wooden cross and taught the Indians about Christ. Spanish missionaries followed in around 1566. They established a network of missions on the islands, converted many of the Guale to Christianity, and settled them in towns, where they would be easier to shepherd and could grow corn for the budding town of St. Augustine. Periodically the Guale rebelled and massacred the priests, but the uprisings were brutally crushed and the missions reëstablished. By 1602 the Church could report 1,200 converts to the faith. It was not a faith nor a way of life that agreed with the Guale, however, and in the course of the next century they would disappear as a people.

Englishmen moving down from settlements in the north encountered the Spanish missions on the Georgia coast. Spain's hold on the coast was tenuous—her real strength was to the south, in Florida—and the Englishmen challenged it. Georgia became one of the more important frontiers in the two centuries of struggle between Spain and England for control of the South. Guale was, in the words of Professor Herbert Bolton, "The Debatable Land." There were decades of raids and reprisals, missions burned and encampments surprised, islands captured and recaptured. Indians did much of the fighting, the tribes changing allegiances when they sensed a shift in the balance of power or when an especially persuasive

English or Spanish agent came among them. The struggle culminated in 1739 in the War of Jenkin's Ear and an English victory.

On the first day of February, 1733, the Englishman Oglethorpe and his band of 114 colonists sailed ten miles up the mouth of a broad river to land on a bluff that rose forty feet above the surrounding grasslands. The white men named the bluff Yamacraw for the red men who lived there. The river was called *Isundiga*, "Bluewater," by the Indians, but the white men gave the river and the town that grew up next to it a name from the Old World, "Savannah," for the grassland stretching away on every side. After displaying his weapons to the Indians, Oglethorpe gathered together the Creek chiefs and the headmen of the small outlying tribes. He spoke to them of the power, wealth, and wisdom of the English nation, and of the many advantages that would come to the Indians from alliance and friendship with that nation. He said finally that as the Indians had plenty of land, he hoped that they would freely resign a share of it for his people who were to come and settle among them for their benefit and instruction. He made the Indians gifts—muskets, knives, and hatchets. He made the promise that the white man would keep his part of the treaty, "as long as the sun shall shine or the waters run in the rivers."

A chief named Tomochichi rose and spoke in the name of the Creek nation.

"Here is a little present; I give you a buffalo's skin adorned on the inside with the head and the feathers of an eagle, which I desire you to accept, because the eagle is a

The Air is found so temperate, and the Seasons of the Year so very regular, that there is no Excess of *Heat*, or *Cold*, nor any sudden Alterations in the Weather; The River Banks are cover'd with a strange Variety of lovely Trees, which being always green, present a thousand Landskips to the Eye, so fine, and so diversified; that the Sight is entirely charm'd with them; the Ground lies sloping towards the Rivers, but, at a Distance, rises gradually, and intermingles little Hills of Wood with fruitful Plains, all cover'd over with wild Flowers, and not a Tree to interrupt the Prospect: Nor is this tempting Country yet inhabited, except those Parts in the Possession of the *English*, unless by here and there a Tribe of wandering *Indians*, wild and ignorant, all artless, and uncultivated, as the Soil, which fosters them.

—Sir Robert Montgomery

symbol of speed, and the buffalo of strength. The English are swift as a bird, and strong as the beast, since like the former they flew over vast seas to the uttermost parts of the earth; and like the latter, they are so strong that nothing can withstand them. The feathers of the eagle are soft, and signify love. The buffalo's skin is warm, signifying protection. Therefore I hope the English will love and protect our little families.''

For this promise of friendship and the protection of George the Second, the Creeks ceded all the land between the Savannah and Ogeechee rivers and all the lands along the seashore down to the St. John's river, except for the islands of Ossapo, Sapala, and Guale, which they reserved for hunting, fishing, and bathing, and a piece of holy ground called the Place of the Pipemakers. When this parchment was dispatched to the colony trustees in London, Oglethorpe mounted cannon in the fort, palisaded the townsite, and began to erect houses. A public garden was started which was designed to supply the settlers with vines, oranges, olives, and other plants from which the trustees might soon begin to realize a profit. To encourage immigration, the colony granted each free male a lot in the town and fifty acres outside it, with the stipulation that at least one hundred mulberry trees be planted to feed the colony's silkworms.

After erecting a ninety-foot beacon on the east end of Tybee Island at the mouth of the Savannah River, Oglethorpe proceeded to erect a chain of fortifications down the coast. Fort Argyle was immediately begun at the mouth of the Ogeechee River, and a stockade and garrison

of marines were placed at Skidaway Narrows to protect the settlement against an invasion from the Spanish at St. Augustine. By 1734 a town and fort were laid out at St. Simons, which was to be called Frederica. By 1735 the town of Augusta was laid out and garrisoned at the site of the "Great Falls," the head of navigation on the Savannah. More than 600 white fur traders were by now living at Fort Moore, downstream on the northern side of the river, and vessels were commissioned, each capable of carrying ten thousand pelts to Charleston. By 1738 the 42nd Oglethorpe's Highland Regiment, from which the "Black Watch" later evolved, had arrived and was headquartered at Fort Frederica. Many of the soldiers brought their families. A settlement and a brewery were begun on Jekyll Island. Forts St. Andrews and Prince William were laid out and under construction on Cumberland, and an outpost was established on the island of Amelia not far north of the St. John's River. In 1738 there were 1,110 colonists in Georgia, exclusive of the few who had come to the colony at their own expense.

Upon the quick failure of the silk, wine, and spice schemes, the settlers turned to cotton, indigo, and the plantation culture. Oglethorpe's forts soon gave way to the settlements of Sunbury, Darien, Brunswick, and St. Mary's. The Indian was steadily pushed westward, river by river, by force and by cession, and soon he came to know what the white man really meant by his treaties lasting, "as long as the sun shall shine or waters run in the rivers." He began to call the white man *Econonoxnoochee*, "He who lusts after the land."

The greatest of the English influences on Georgia was the plantation culture, transported westward to the barrier islands from the West Indies, where it had begun.

The West Indian islands of Barbados and Jamaica were rich in sugar and tobacco plantations when the colonies of Plymouth and Jamestown were struggling to survive to the north. Word got out about the fecundity of the West Indies, too many Englishmen came, and the prices fell. The wealthiest planters in Barbados commissioned Commander William Hilton to search out a new land suitable for the plantation culture. Commander Hilton, on concluding his search, recommended the section of mainland coast from 31° to 33°45' north, and that land became "Carolina." (The territory called Georgia would be carved from it sixty-three years later.) Twelve hundred Barbados residents arrived in 1670 and settled at Charlestown, where they continued in the way of life begun in the West Indies.

The English had brought English order to Jamaica and to Barbados, dividing the land into parishes and laying out towns within the parishes, and here on the Carolina coast they did the same, marking out parishes and establishing the towns of Charleston, Savannah, Sunbury, Brunswick, and St. Mary's. Rice was introduced to Carolina in 1694, and indigo somewhat later. "Sea Island" cotton came in the late eighteenth century from the West Indies, where it had grown wild. Plantations grew up on the coast of Georgia and the Carolinas—Valambrossa, Silk Hope, Wormsloe, Cedar Grove, Middleplace, Laurel Hill, Orange Grove, Hopeton, Hofwyl, Wildhorn, Lee Hall, Dungeness, and Retreat. Long before they flourished, however, there had existed, in the tobacco and sugar and indigo plantations of Barbados and Jamaica, the plantation model and all its appurtenances, the "big house," outbuildings, field hands, "drivers," white overseers, house hands, runaways, superannuation, whipping.

Plantation culture in all its expressions—its architecture, agricultural methods, slave codes, and economics—flourished in all of Carolina, but reached its peak and epitome on the Golden Isles of Georgia. The Sea Island cotton from Retreat Plantation on St. Simons Island was finer than any other long staple cotton in the South, and it brought seven more cents a pound on the London and Liverpool markets; and so in all things was the Georgia coast always a little more so.

"I was fain to think I had landed on some one of those fairy islands said to have existed in the Golden Age," James Audubon wrote of his arrival at Retreat Plantation in 1831. Sea captains brought tubs of trees to Retreat from all over the world. A tabby greenhouse was built to accommodate them, and in time it became the center of a famous arboretum. East of the house was a U-shaped garden in which ninety-two varieties of rose bloomed along with honeysuckles, honeyflowers, verbenas, phlox, and nasturtiums, all sheltered by a windbreak of osage oranges, crepe myrtle, and oleander. In the shade of these trees sat three latticed summerhouses. There were citrus and olive groves, peach and pear orchards, grape arbors, fig trees in four varieties, and a huge vegetable garden. Pecan trees edged the road, black walnuts shaded the quarters for the house hands, and mulberry trees surrounded the chicken yard. It is still said on St. Simons that the sailors of those days could smell the fragrance of Retreat from twelve miles out.

Not every visitor was charmed by the life on island plantations. Frances Kemble, one of the great English actresses of her day, married a wealthy sea-island planter and moved to the Georgia coast in 1838. She was so appalled by the fact of slavery that her stay in Georgia, and her marriage as well, lasted for only a few months after her arrival. Twenty-two years later she published in England her anti-slavery *Journal of a Residence on a Georgian Plantation*, a book whose merits are still warmly debated on the coast. Georgia's society shocked Fanny Kemble, but Georgia's land soothed. Sometimes for Fanny, as for Audubon seven years before, the islands were fairy islands.

"I am helped to bear all that is so very painful to me here," she wrote, "by my constant enjoyment of the strange, wild scenery in the midst of which I live, and which my resumption of my equestrian habits gives me almost daily opportunity of observing. I rode today to some new-cleared and plowed ground that was being prepared for the precious cotton crop. I crossed a salt marsh upon a raised causeway that was perfectly alive with land crabs, whose desperately active endeavors to avoid my horse's hoofs were so ludicrous that I literally laughed alone and aloud at them. The sides of this road across the swamp were covered with a thick and close embroidery of creeping moss, or rather lichens of the most vivid green and red: the latter made my horse's path look as if it was edged with an exquisite pattern of coral; it was like a thing in a fairy tale, and delighted me extremely."

Not all Europeans lusted after the Georgia land. Ten years before Oglethorpe and his colonists arrived in the New World with their visions of wealth from silk and spices, there came another Englishman, Mark Catesby, with a different sort of vision. Past the sites where Oglethorpe would build forts in fear, the tall, quiet Catesby traveled in perfect calm on his way upriver into the wilderness. He disappeared for months at a time beyond the last trading post at Fort Moore, armed only with his watercolors and sometimes accompanied by an Indian.

Catesby had heard the Cherokees speak of their own garden of Eden, "the vales of Keowe," at the headwaters of the Savannah River, and he set out in search of the place. It was probably in the summer of 1724 that he arrived there. He saw, along the headwater riverbanks, catalpa and water ash underlain by thickets of flowering rhododendron and mountain laurel, which gave way above the banks to a vast virgin forest of oaks interspersed with stands of tall hickories and hemlocks. The tree limbs were heavy with chattering gray-and-red passenger pigeons that came to feast on the mast. "Of these," Catesby wrote, "there come in the winter to Virginia and to Carolina, from the North, incredible numbers; insomuch that in some places where they roost, which they do on one another's backs, they often break down limbs of oaks with their weight and leave their dung some inches thicker under the trees they roost on. Where they light, they so effectually clear the woods of acorns and other mast that the Hogs that come after them, to the detriment of the planters, fare very poorly. In Virginia I have seen them fly in such continued trains three days successively, that there was not the least interval in loosing sight of them." In the understory Catesby found the flowering *Stuartia*, a close relative of the oriental camellia, along with copses of dogwood, with borders often traced by the Indian pink, whose scarlet flowers shot up like roman candles. He marveled at the run of spawning sturgeons as they leapt the rapids at the fall line and passed over into still waters, where each female laid her more than two million eggs.

Catesby painted his creatures against a background of the flowers or trees they frequented. He sketched the yellow swallowtail butterfly flitting among the branches of the water ash, and the cedar waxwing around the crimson sweetshrub. He drew the luna moth hovering about the delicate, snowy *Philadelphus*, and he perched the parula warbler on the limb of the silverbell tree.

After two years of wandering in the "Carolina" wilderness, and a year of sketching fish in the Bahamas, Catesby returned to London in 1725 to etch, watercolor, and bind a book of the things he had seen. The great work,

which took him nearly twenty years to complete, was issued in sections as he completed them. The first twenty plates were presented to the Royal Society in 1729. The first volume was finished and presented to the Society, which by now had admitted Catesby as a member, in 1732, several months before Georgia became a proprietary colony. The book bore the heroic title, *The Natural History of Carolina, Florida, and the Bahama Islands; Containing the Figures of Birds, Beasts, Fishes, Serpents, Insects, and Plants: Particularly, the Forest-Trees, Shrubs, and Other Plants, Not Hitherto Described, or Very Incorrectly Figured by Authors. Together with Their Descriptions in English and French. To Which Are Added Observations on the Air, Soil, and Water; with Remarks upon Agriculture, Grain, Pulse, Roots, Etc. To the Whole is Prefixed a New and Correct Map of the Countries Treated of,* and was dedicated to Queen Caroline, for whom the colony was named. For the first volume Catesby, working alone, prepared the 100 copper etchings and engraved and watercolored the 10,000 plates of the first printing of 1,000 copies. Eleven years later he finished the 112 plates of the second volume, and three years after this effort he died. He had produced the first illustrated American ornithology, and was the first illustrator to paint his birds against the background of their feeding and nesting vegetation.

Several years after Catesby's death, his work came to the attention of an American farmer named John Bartram, "the greatest botanist in the New World," according to Linnaeus. Bartram lived on the banks of the Schulykill River near Philadelphia, and there maintained the most extensive botanical garden in America while corresponding with Linnaeus in Sweden, Peter Collinson in England, Benjamin Franklin, and other naturalists. Bartram, upon receiving a set of Catesby's *Natural History* from Collinson, was so inspired by its contents that he decided to set out on the Catesby Trail. Commissioned the King's botanist, he began his first expedition at Charleston in 1760, and on this and a later trip he traveled across Carolina, up the Savannah River, and on down the Georgia coast into Florida, discovering new plants and birds and recording them in his *Diary of a Journey Through the Carolinas, Georgia, and Florida*. His son William, who went along on the second trip, was caught up by the beauty, and seven years later he set out on the first of three long journeys of his own, beginning in 1773 and ending with the start of the American Revolution, which he joined. The account of his botanical odyssey through much of the Southeast was published in Philadelphia in 1791 as *Travels Through North and South Carolina, Georgia, East and West Florida*.

William Bartram's writing was not so spare and Quaker-plain as his father's. William was one of the traveling writer-naturalists whose reports from the frontiers of the New World were being read voraciously in Europe, and the son was more aware of his audience. As a naturalist he

William Bartram: Prairie warbler and shell

was less a descendant of his father John than of William Dampier, the seventeenth-century pirate whose journals influenced Defoe and Swift. Of Dampier and the other founders of their school, Loren Eiseley writes, "Not alone did the reading of voyages become popular, but the rough-hewn voyagers themselves began to respond to the demand for greater accuracy and more dispassionate accounts of peoples and places visited. . . . Pirates and sea dogs were becoming the unacknowledged agents of the Royal Society. The truth that was wanted, however, was novel truth, truth of far lands, new faunas, peoples, and customs." William Bartram was among the progenitors of Hooker, Lyell, and Darwin, and of the revolution that these observant travelers brought to natural science.

"Desirous of visiting the islands," William wrote of one trip to the coast, "I forded a narrow shoal, part of the sound, and landed on one of them, which employed me the whole day to explore. The surface and vegetable mould here is generally a loose sand, not very fertile, except some spots bordering on the sound and inlets, where are found heaps or mounds of sea-shell, either formerly brought there, by the Indians, who inhabited the island, or which

were perhaps thrown up in ridges, by the beating surface of the sea: possibly both these circumstances may have contributed to their formation. These sea-shells, through length of time, and the subtle penetrating effects of the air, which dissolve them to earth, render these ridges very fertile, and which, when clear of their trees, and cultivated, become profusely productive of almost every kind of vegetable. Here are also large plantations of indigo, corn, and potatoes, with many other sorts of esculent plants. I observed, amongst the shells of the conical mounds, fragments of earthen vessels, and of other utensils, the manufacture of the ancients: about the centre of one of them, the rim of an earthen pot appeared amongst the shells and earth, which I carefully removed, and drew it out, almost whole: this pot was curiously wrought all over the outside, representing basket work, and was undoubtedly esteemed a very ingenious performance, by the people, at the age of its construction.

"The upper surface, or vegetative soil of the island, lies on a foundation, or stratum, of tenacious cinereous coloured clay, which perhaps is the principal support of the vast growth of timber that arises from the surface, which is little more than a mixture of fine white sand and dissolved vegetables, serving as a nursery bed to hatch, or bring into existence, the infant plant, and to supply it with aliment and food, suitable to its delicacy and tender frame, until the roots, acquiring sufficient extent and solidity to lay hold of the clay, soon attain a magnitude and stability sufficient to maintain its station. Probably if this clay were dug out, and cast upon the surface, after

William Bartram: Great golden speckled bream

being meliorated by the saline or nitrous qualities of the air, it would kindly incorporate with the loose sand, and become a productive and lasting manure.

William Bartram: Alegator

"The roebuck, or deer, are numerous on this island; the tyger, wolf, and bear, hold yet some possession; as also raccoons, foxes, hares, squirrels, rats and mice, but I think no moles; there is a large ground-rat, more than twice the size of the common Norway rat. In the night time, it throws out the earth, forming little mounds, or hillocks. Opposoms are here in abundance, as also pole-cats, wild-cats, rattlesnakes, glass-snake, coach-whip snake, and a variety of other serpents. Here are also a great variety of birds, throughout the seasons, inhabiting both sea and land. First I shall name the eagle, of which there are three species: the great grey eagle is the largest, of great strength and high flight; he chiefly preys on fawns and other young quadrupeds.

"The bald eagle is likewise a large, strong, and very active bird, but an execrable tyrant: he supports his assumed dignity and grandeur by rapine and violence, extorting unreasonable tribute and subsidy from all the feathered nations."

In the Georgia swamps Bartram encountered the alligator:

"Behold him rushing forth from the flags and reeds. His enormous body swells. His plaited tail brandished high, floats upon the lake. The waters like a cataract descend from his opening jaws. Clouds of smoke issue from his dilated nostrils. The earth trembles with his thunder. When immediately from the opposite coast of the lagoon, emerges from the deep his rival champion. They suddenly dart upon each other. The boiling surface of the lake marks their rapid course, and a terrific conflict commences. They now sink to the bottom folded together in horrid wreaths. The water becomes thick and discoloured. Again they rise, their jaws clap together, re-echoing through the deep surrounding forests. Again they sink, when the contest ends at the muddy bottom of the lake, and the vanquished makes a hazardous escape, hiding himself in the muddy turbulent waters and sedge on a distant shore. The proud victor exulting returns to the place of action. The shores

How shall I express myself so as to convey an adequate idea of it to the reader, and at the same time avoid raising suspicions of my want of veracity. Should I say, that the river (in this place) from shore to shore, and perhaps near half a mile above and below me, appeared to be one solid bank of fish, of various kinds, pushing through this narrow pass of St. Juans into the little lake, on their return down the river, and that the alligators were in such incredible numbers, and so close together from shore to shore, that it would have been easy to have walked across on their heads, had the animals been harmless. What expressions can sufficiently declare the shocking scene that for some minutes continued, whilst this mighty army of fish were forcing the pass? During this attempt, thousands, I may say hundreds of thousands of them were caught and swallowed by the devouring alligators. I have seen an alligator take up out of the water several great fish at a time, and just squeeze them betwixt his jaws, while the tails of the great trout flapped about his eyes and lips, ere he had swallowed them. The horrid noise of their closing jaws, their plunging amidst the broken banks of fish, and rising with their prey some feet upright above the water, the floods of water and blood rushing out of their mouths, and the clouds of vapour issuing from their wide nostrils, were truly frightful. This scene continued at intervals during the night, as the fish came to the pass. After this sight, shocking and tremendous as it was, I found myself somewhat easier and more reconciled to my situation, being convinced that their extraordinary assemblage here, was owing to this annual feast of fish, and that they were so well employed in their own element, that I had little occasion to fear their paying me a visit.

—WILLIAM BARTRAM

and forests resound his dreadful roar, together with the triumphing shouts of the plaited tribes around, witnesses of the horrid combat.''

In 1785 the famous French botanist André Michaux was commissioned by the French government to undertake an expedition to North America, to explore and gather examples of flora which might benefit France. After a brief interlude in the country around New York, Michaux and his son François disembarked at Charleston in 1786, to spend the next ten years crossing the Appalachians and journeying widely across the American frontier, from Canada to Louisiana. He gathered 60,000 trees and plants for shipment back to France, few of which survived, unfortunately, the excesses of the French Revo-

lution. Before publishing any record of his journeys in the heart of America, Michaux departed on an expedition to the East Indies, where he died in 1802. It was left to his son to edit and publish his two-volume work on North American flora and a third book on American oaks. As William Bartram had done, François Michaux returned to follow in the footsteps of his father, and he produced one of the most popular and enduring accounts of the area. His *Voyage à l'ouest des Monts Alléganys* was so popular that it appeared in French, German, and English editions. His *Histoire des Arbres Forestiers de l'Amérique Septentrionale* displayed a keen understanding of the interrelationships in the forest and the necessity for conservation there, and earned him the title "Father of American Forestry."

The populations of animals are dense and seasonal. At times there are population explosions when thousands of dragon-flies swarm over the fresh-water ponds and meadows; when a walk through the orchards stirs up clouds of small brown moths which flutter like bits of paper ash in the wind; when sand flies and mosquitoes swarm out of the marshes by the millions to make the few humans feel unimportant and miserable.

—MILDRED and JOHN TEAL

The boy smelled the spice of crushed fern as he walked. Over its aroma lay the lighter odour of palmetto bloom. He divided them in his nostrils, the one from the other.

—MARJORIE RAWLINGS

Swamp at Mule Run, Ossabaw (John Earl)

The little grass frog, so delicate one can nearly see through his body, is a member of the tree frog or tree toad family, creatures which have adhesive disks on their toes to help them climb. We first heard their tiny, high-pitched calls coming from the grass in a roadside drainage ditch. Name any frustrating experience, and the finding of this frog equals it. We crouched as close as we dared to the ditch from which the noise was coming, pointed the flashlight and turned it on. The chirping continued for a moment and then stopped, and we saw nothing but grass. We turned off the light, moved to another spot, wildly brushing off mosquitoes, and waited for the sound to begin again. This was repeated again and again; and it was only later, after we had given up and then returned, that we saw, not at water level where one naturally looks for frogs, but up on the leaves of grass, frogs so tiny that their weight didn't bend the grass. This smallest of North American frogs uses grass as a substitute for trees, and climbs up perhaps fifty body lengths, that is two feet, from the ground.

   The tree frogs, taken together, are much more numerous than the typical pond frogs; and it was the former that made most of the noise. After a rain on a warm night we were awed at the thought that so much noise could be produced by such tiny creatures.

. . .

The chicks hatched in three to four weeks. Baby herons are somewhat intermediate between the completely helpless and naked song-bird young and the active, downy young of turkeys, gulls, and shore-birds. Young herons have a scraggly down covering, but can move very little after hatching. It would be dangerous for them to do so because they might fall or damage the nest. They sit still, trying to look as unobtrusive as possible and failing completely. The little balls of green skin covered by the moth-eaten-looking white fuzz stand out clearly against the leaves and branches, especially since the nests must be exposed to allow the large adults a clear landing.

The young birds have very unpleasant personal habits, which are accentuated when the birds are disturbed. The most pugnacious creatures were the young black-crowned night herons. A weighing sequence usually went like this: As we approached the nest, the young vomited their last meal with considerable vigor and good aim. Since the meal might have consisted of a nine-inch mullet, the intruder was dealt quite a blow.

—MILDRED and JOHN TEAL

Baby egrets, Ossabaw Island rookery

Bull Street, Savannah

There are no more passenger pigeons in Georgia's Eden —or any place. The fur traders departed soon after the birds, and are now centuries gone. The plantation life lasted longer, but it too has departed. On the coast it died gracefully. In 1863, after Retreat Plantation had been abandoned for two years, Union Colonel Thomas Higginson visited it and wrote a sort of epitaph: "The air had that peculiar Mediterranean translucency which southern islands wear, and the plantation we visited had the loveliest tropical garden, though tangled and desolate, which I have ever seen in the South. The deserted house was embowered in great blossoming shrubs and filled with hyacinthine odors, among which predominated that of the little Chickasaw roses which everywhere bloomed and trailed around."

The old plantation life has left only traces—as at Hofwyl, where a massive mahogany four-postered bed dominates one room, above it navy blue, bubbled glass windows with green louvered shutters brought from Barbados. There are old letters of the sort that now, a century later, permit just the memory of memories: "Your grandfather, George Columbus Dent, and I were married in the old Broadfield house on the 22nd of November 1847 by the Rev. T. Longfellow Smith. The first eight years (the winters I mean) of our married life were passed at Cedar Hill, near Darien, with your father's grandmother Dent. At her death in 1856 we moved over to Broadfield and Hofwyl was settled, your grandfather calling it after the great Hofwyl School in Switzerland (Professor Fredenberg) where he had been educated. From all I hear it does not stand as it stood. The house at Hofwyl was not finished when our Civil War broke out and we left, for some years living in Ware County near Waycross, a miserable wiregrass country. Before we returned, the extinguishing cap of defeat on our heads, our pleasant things all gone, strangers were in our homes. I must close now. You can arrange these crude pages to suit yourself— it is only an old woman's recollections."

Vestiges of the African half of plantation culture persist today. The language called Gullah, or Geechee, is still spoken by a few coastal people. Its words are now mostly English, but its rhythms are African. A number of Gullah words have escaped from the coast and have entered the American language. All sons of the South have heard of biddies—baby chickens. The word is derived from *bidibidi*, which in the language of the Kongo people of Angola means "bird." "Cooter," slang in the South for turtle, comes from the Bambara word for turtle, *kuta*. "Goober," comes from *nguba*, the Kimbundu word for peanut. Most coastal men have at one time or another toted a croker sack of yams. *Tota* in Kongo means to pick up. Croker is a west African word, and yam comes from *yambi*, a Mende word from Sierra Leone. "Tabby," the beautiful coastal building material made of oyster shells, lime, and sand, comes from a Wolof word describing houses made of a similar material in Senegal. "Juke box" comes from a Wolof word for music. The Uncle Remus stories are African folk stories modified for coastal animal heroes.

Guale was for a short time a black separatist nation, the first and only such experiment in the history of the United States. In 1865, at the request of a man named Tunis Campbell and eighteen other black leaders, General Sherman issued Headquarters Order Number 15, which established a black empire, "from the islands from Charleston South, the abandoned rice fields along the rivers for 30 miles back from the sea and the country bordering on the St. Johns River, Florida.

". . . on the islands and in the settlements hereafter to be established, no white persons whatever, unless military officers and soldiers detached for duty, will be permitted to reside; and the sale and exclusive management of affairs will be left to the freed people themselves, subject only to the United States military and Acts of Congress."

The U.S. government considered Order Number 15 no more binding than its treaties with Indians, apparently, for within two years most of the land on St. Catherines Island, the capital of the new nation, was sold to Northern speculators. A small black army resisted the carpetbaggers for a time, then surrendered to Federal troops.

The English and the African are the dominant human influences on this coast. They are past their prime, but are lingering. A new culture impinges, a culture that future historians may well find less grand and interesting than what went before. It does not fall to ruins as fragrant as those Colonel Higginson smelled on St. Simons, nor are its rhythms as haunting as the African Gullah.

North of Kingsland there is a garage surrounded by the carcasses of rusting automobiles, with yearling pines pushing through open hoods and broken back windows. The names are still there in chrome: Biscayne, Bel Aire, Grand Prix, Holiday, Dynamic 88, Galaxie 500, Catalina, Starliner, Monterey, Chieftain, Apache. A small boy emerges from among the wrecks and recites the history of each. "That's the Kingsland Police patrol car. They lost control chasing a drunk, ran right through two telephone poles which squeezed it together. Two were killed in the gray VW. The last thing the lady said before she died was, 'Where's my little dog?' You wanna see Tommy Close's wrecked stock car?"

The people who came first left least. We know very little of the Guale, "the people of the land and sea," the aboriginal inhabitants of this coast. We know more of the Cusabo, who lived above the Guale, and the Timucua, who lived below them. We have no extensive record of Guale language, customs, or taboos. We *do* have giant shell heaps on Cane Patch Island off Ossabaw, and arrowheads on Cumberland, and burial mounds on St. Catherines, and tiny middens everywhere. We have the names of rivers, Ogeechee, Canoochee, Ohoopee, Sapelo, Ocmulgee, Oconee, Altamaha, and of islands, Wassaw, Ossabaw, Guale, Sapelo, Missoe, and of lost towns, Aleguifa, Osao, Fosquiche, Sotequa, Talapa, Tupiqui, Tulufina, Utine. But that is all we have. A pure substance burns without leaving ash. In Georgia the people who left the least impression are perhaps the most impressive.

5. The Sea Island Singers

For many a mile [on the Altamaha] we saw no habitations, and the solitude was profound;
but our black oarsmen made the woods echo to their song. One of them taking the lead,
first improvised a verse, paying compliments to his master's family, and to a celebrated
black beauty of the neighborhood, who was compared to the "red bird." The other five then
joined in chorus, always repeating the same words. Occasionally they struck up a hymn,
taught them by the Methodists, in which the most sacred subjects were handled with strange
familiarity, and which, though nothing irreverent was meant, sounded oddly to our ears . . .

—SIR CHARLES LYELL

John Davis of St. Simons Island is sixty-five and has been ill lately, but he is still built like an organ. You can tell what a rich person he is by the sound of his voice. There's a mile of song in his one baritone word, even in the "well," with which he begins each of his stories and songs. St. Simons is a small island but it has a continent's store of music, and John Davis, by authority of his voice, is its crown prince or its Buddha. John lives in a tiny, ten by ten foot clapboard hut in the Harrington section of St. Simons, where black people have owned freeholds since slavery. His old bungalow and all his earthly possessions burned recently, and the rust and ash of the ruins stand next to his new hut.

One afternoon of the October after the fire, the Sea Island Singers, the most venerable singing group in the islands, gathered at John's place. "Convened" would be the wrong word, for the singers left their own homes when the spirit moved them and they arrived at John's in their own time. Bessie Jones, the soprano, and Emma Lee Ramsey, the alto, came early. The bass, John's brother Jerome Davis, came late—almost at dusk. The Sea Island Singers are not slick entertainers. Sometimes, before an audience, a singing session never really gets started but the Singers have to begin anyway—show business. At home it is never that way. "Spirituals don't just start," John explains. "Spirituals were the spirit of folks in slavery. They sang to revive their spirit and to keep from having to think about their task. You don't just begin to

sing about that. That's what's wrong with most places who hire us. They want us to come and sing and leave, and sometimes they even want to tell us what to sing. That's when it never gets started. You just can't do that. Every day I got a tune. The next day it's different. A song's got a tune to it and we sing 'em as they come. We do the things we learned as children."

So they didn't just begin, on that warm October afternoon near dusk. Instead they talked, sitting on the bed and the floor and on John's several rickety chairs, almost touching one another. They joked, laughed, bantered. They told a story or two, and each singer expressed his state of mind through parables. In good time, Bessie turned and said, "Sing 'Moses', John."

"You're the last one to come off a tour," John answered. "Let me start with you till I can get my voice together."

Bessie Jones has an oval face and a great body full of music. She leaves St. Simons often to go on tour, for she is the world's most sought-after singer of true coastal music. ("I don't sing 'jump-ups,' just the real songs of the coast," she says.) She lives in a bungalow off Harlem Lane, at the end of a sandy path marked by two Chinaberry trees. She is a lay preacher at Harlem Lane Baptist Church, which is pastored by her son, and she is the author of *Step It Down*, a book of coastal song. On her bungalow wall is a new calendar photograph of Kennedy, Kennedy, and King; in her memory are the old riddles, songs, dances, and stories she learned as a child from her grandfather, who came from Africa when he was seven with rings in his ears and wore his hair plaited until he died in 1942, at the age of 105. Nowadays Bessie sings coastal lullabies to *her* grandchildren—to her "grands" as coastal black people say—who repay her when they are older by doing the 'jump for joy,' a dance that the rest of the country now calls the Charleston.

At John's place that afternoon, Bessie spoke to herself a little before launching into the song. Her tambourine filled the small hut with its sound. It was nearly dark, but things were starting at last. John picked up the tune, tried the first line of "You go down brother Moses," decided he liked it, and sang the whole song with the others joining in on the refrain.

You go down a' brother Moses,
way down in Egypt land.
Tell ol' King Pharaoh,
tell him to let my children go.
Oh, tell him to go down a' brother Moses,
go way down there in Egypt land.
Won't you tell ol' King Pharaoh,
tell him to let my children go?

Then came one spiritual after another. "Moses," "Goodbye and fare you well" or "I ain't gonna be here long," and then "Beulah land," its quick beat accompanied by bass and tenor clapping, and then the work song "Riley." John explained that this last is really a sailor's work song. At the turn of the century sailing ships, sometimes as many as eighty, stood at Darien and Brunswick waiting to load and carry away timber from the great slash-pine forests of south Georgia. In the voices of the Sea Island Singers a listener can feel the sailors pulling, resting, pulling at anchor chain or sail.

If I hadda known that the boss was blind,
Oh Riley, oh man,
I wouldn't go to work till half past nine.
Goodbye my Riley oh.
I wish I was the captain's son,
Oh Riley, oh man,
I'd set on the bank and drink good rum.
Goodbye my Riley oh.

John sang his favorite storytelling song, "Nineteen hundred and forty-two," an epic that describes the whole of the Second World War. Everyone joined him in a song about the sinking of the *Titanic*, then in two shout songs, "Walk believer, walk," and "Blow Gabriel, blow."

The coffee can of water on top of the coal-oil register began to vibrate, and with that, as if it were a signal, the singing stopped and the storytelling began.

Cumberland Island

The Live Oaks are of an astonishing magnitude, and one tree contains a prodigious quantity of timber, yet comparatively, they are not tall, even in these forests, where growing on strong land, in company with others of great altitude (such as Fagus sylvatica, Liquid-amber, Magnolia grandiflora, and the high Palm tree) they strive while young to be upon an equality with their neighbours, and to enjoy the influence of the sun-beams, and of the pure animating air; but the others at last prevail, and their proud heads are seen at a great distance, towering far above the rest of the forest. The trunk of the Live Oak is generally from twelve to eighteen feet in girt, and rises ten or twelve feet erect from the earth; some I have seen eighteen or twenty; then divides itself into three, four, or five great limbs, which continue to grow in nearly an horizontal direction, each limb forming a gentle curve, or arch, from its base to its extremity. I have stepped above fifty paces, on a strait line, from the trunk of one of these trees, to the extremity of the limbs. They are ever green, and the wood almost incorruptible, even in the open air. It bears a prodigious quantity of fruit; the acorn is small, but sweet and agreeable to the taste when roasted, and is food for almost all animals. The Indians obtain from it a sweet oil, which they use in the cooking of hommony, rice, &c. and they also roast them in hot embers, eating them as we do chesnuts.

—JOHN BARTRAM

Trees were gentle. The sounds they made were lovely sounds. The susurrus of the palms, the sibilance of the pines, the roar and rush of great winds through the oaks and magnolias, were the only music she had known.

—MARJORIE RAWLINGS

The trees are massive and beautiful. Some branches of the biggest ones may push themselves out forty feet from the trunk and nearly reach the ground with a few gnarled dips. The crown, the branches and leafy area of the tree, is usually much wider than it is high. The leaves, which are small, egg-shaped, smooth, tough, and shiny, grow in profusion, and they give the tree its name, live oak, because they remain evergreen. There is a general leaf fall in the spring; there is a sound like the sound of rain as the crisp leaves tick down and blow along the ground. The leaves that fall are the older ones. The young ones remain firmly in place. The leaf cover on the forest floor at this time may be two or three inches thick.

. . .

An oak tree is an island unto itself, providing both soil and water.
The bark is very rough and deeply grooved. Along the lower, big branches,
the bark catches and retains moisture. With time, a little dust and leaf
mold accumulate in the wet grooves, soon making a fine soil, a kind of mulch,
which is fertile territory for seeds or plants that are blown onto the branches.
Even small trees, especially oak and palmetto, grow in the forks of the live
oak trees. Resurrection fern takes to this dust and leaf mold especially well,
and the ferns line the lower branches of most trees. The fern is green and
erect during the humid, warm summers. It shrivels to gray curls during the
cold, relatively dry winters, and expands again with the arrival of spring.

Live oak and resurrection ferns, Cumberland

There is an old saying that a live oak takes a hundred years to grow, lives for a hundred years, and then takes another hundred years to die.

—MILDRED and JOHN TEAL

He was astonished that she knew none of the trees of the hammock except the magnolia and the holly. He pointed them out and described their peculiarities, so that she would surely know them again. Red bay and sweet bay, sweet gum and ironwood—She followed his finger with her grave eyes. He stopped in his tracks and looked at her.

"What's wild mulberry good for?" he asked her sternly.

"Why—I suppose the birds eat the fruit."

"They ain't no finer wood in the world for oar-lock blocks," he informed her solemnly.

Every tree fitted into his life. Its beauty and its purpose were joined together, so that the most beautiful trees to him were those with the greatest use. For the slim white ash trees he felt a tenderness, gauging their probable length in terms of strands for firing in the furnace of his still. Near the Twin Sinks he led her up the ledge to the two giant hickories. He walked around and around them, warming to their straightness and good grain.

"They's hundreds o' feet o' timber in each o' them hickories," he said proudly. "I don't aim to cut 'em lest I got it to do. Trees like that is scarce."

She tipped her head back and stared submissively at the tops, where the leaves hung golden against the blue translucent sky.

. . .

Below the hickories again, where the hammock merged with swamp, he cut a low-growing palmetto. He trimmed down the ivory cylinder that was the heart of the palm and cut a shaving from the lower end, where the fan-like sections fitted intricately together. They tasted it. It was crisp and sweet, like chestnuts.

"That's a swamp cabbage that's fitten," he decided.

—MARJORIE RAWLINGS

They tell us that plants are perishable, soulless creatures, that only man is immortal, etc.; but this, I think, is something that we know very nearly nothing about. Anyhow, this palm was indescribably impressive and told me grander things than I ever got from human priest.

This vegetable has a plain gray shaft, round as a broom-handle, and a crown of varnished channeled leaves. It is a plainer plant than the humblest of Wisconsin oaks; but, whether rocking and rustling in the wind or poised thoughtful and calm in the sunshine, it has a power of expression not excelled by any plant high or low that I have met in my whole walk thus far.

—JOHN MUIR

As we approached the sea and the brackish water, the wood bordering the river began first to grow dwarfish, and then, lowering suddenly, to give place entirely to reeds; but still we saw the buried stumps and stools of the cypress and pine continuing to show themselves in every section of the bank, maintaining the upright position in which they originally grew. The occurrence of these in the salt marshes clearly demonstrates that trees once flourished where they would now be immediately killed by the salt water. There must have been a change in the relative level of land and sea, to account for their growth, since, even above the commencement of the brackish water, similar stumps are visible at a lower level than the present high tide, and covered by layers of sedimentary matter, on which tall cypresses and other trees are now standing. From such phenomena we may infer the following sequence of events:—first, an ancient forest was submerged several feet, and the sunk trees were killed by the salt water; they then rotted away down to the water level (a long operation), after which layers of sand were thrown down upon the stumps; and finally, when the surface had been raised by fluviatile sediment, as in a delta, a new forest grew up over the ruins of the old one.

—SIR CHARLES LYELL

Palmettos in evening light, Ossabaw

Storm cloud, Cumberland

The oak would look old by itself even without the addition of Spanish moss, or "Old Man's Beard," but the moss ages the tree until it looks like Rip Van Winkle after his long sleep. The moss hangs in great festoons, which may be so long and thick as to mute sound and still the air in the forests.

—MILDRED and JOHN TEAL

Oak, Spanish moss, and grapevine, Ossabaw

6. Sarah Grant

The only way to get to "Fuskie," as the island is called by its natives, is on the rickety O.E.O. mailboat that runs from Savannah on three days a week, or from Bluffton, South Carolina, on two. It is difficult to find the dock from which the mailboat leaves Savannah, for there really is no dock, just a place where the boat ties up to several old piles beside the bank of the Savannah. Daufuskie is a lost island, unknown to many inhabitants of coastal Georgia, or known only vaguely, in name. (At almost any grocery store on the coast you can buy "Daufuskie Brand" oysters in a vermilion can with an Indian in full head-dress on the label.) No sign says "Boat to Daufuskie." If you go to River Street, though, and walk down next to the river and look down the long lane of cobblestones brought here long ago as ballast in sailing ships, you will see a tall sycamore tree. The sycamore marks the spot. By 2:30 of any Saturday afternoon, Captain Willy Simmons and his mates Thomas Stafford and Joe Bryan will be under the tree readying the *Maybe*, as the mailboat is called by some Fuskians, for its return voyage down the Savannah and up what the maps call the Intercoastal Waterway and older Fuskie people call Florida Passage; a hour-and-a-half trip through marshlands that stretch away to either side, broken occasionally by islet-copses of palmettos, pines, and oaks.

Maybe the *Maybe* will run, and maybe she won't. Often she won't. She is a gray, loaf-shaped vessel with a stern that rides low because of rot and seepage. The stamped brass plate inside her tiny cabin reads: "U.S. Army 37 ft. Patrol Boat Built by the Matthews Company Port Clinton Ohio No. J3585—1951." "The battery's run down," is a common complaint, and it comes usually after the bilge pump has been operating all night to keep the boat afloat.

On boat days preceding Christmas it is possible to spot the Daufuskie non-dock by the crowd of people gathering there. By three in the afternoon, the shore beneath the sycamore is in confusion as dusty taxis arrive, exploding with linoleum rugs, lengths of steel, gray tin stove pipes, toys, cases of beer, groceries, plows. Captain Willy Simmons directs the loading, trying to keep the *Maybe* in balance. Some of the baggage arrives on the top of heads, each bundle balanced with one hand while the other holds a boxed lunch to be eaten on the way across the water. Many of the island's high-school students (the school on Daufuskie goes only through the eighth grade) gather here to go home for Christmas. Amid much laughter, drinking, and scuffling, the vessel is finally loaded. The engine starts on the first try if everyone is lucky and the *Maybe* swings out into the Savannah.

Daufuskie is an island of ox carts and sandy roads, great live oaks draped with moss, old bungalows with faded Kelly-green shutters, wood stoves, iron bedsteads painted white, silver marsh mists, musk red island sun-sets, fishing, net repairing, the sea. Daufuskie's older memories are of working long ago in island rice fields or crossing the Florida Passage in the sloop *Messenger Boy* to sell island produce at the old market in Savannah. Dau-fuskie's breakfasts are of fried mullet, pullet eggs, and coffee; its dinners, the more festive ones at least, are served under festooned oaks, the moss illuminated by homemade kerosene lanterns—wicks of twisted paper stuck into narrow-necked bottles—casting a light that you can smell. The light falls yellow on tables piled high with blue enamelled pans of deviled crabs, cloth-covered bowls of boiled shrimp, platters of tiny biscuits filled with ham and sausage, baskets of fresh berries and blueberry dump-lings, and bowls of rice. On the way back through the night smells and indigo darkness of the marshland, the conversation falls into the rhythm of the ox cart on the sandy road, a rhythm interrupted only briefly for a stop at a clear, spring-fed pool so that the ox can drink, then re-suming with the driver's stern ox command. The lights of

Savannah appear on the horizon, and a crescent moon and a single star show above the black, long-needled slash pines.

"We drove home by moonlight," wrote Fannie Kemble nearly a century and a half ago (certain things have changed very little in Guale), "and as we came towards the woods in the middle of the island, the fireflies glittered out from the dusky thickets, as if some magical golden veil was every now and then shaken out into the darkness. The air was enchantingly mild and soft, and the whole way through the silvery night, delightful."

The road to Sarah Grant's house on Daufuskie has writing on it—worm scribblings, the bounding quotation marks of deer, snake slithers, centipede wanderings. The worms have the most to say. Their task is to loosen the soil, let air and water in, and turn the earth over so that it can spring again. Theirs is a monumental reshaping, and the energy for it is only hinted at in the crazy scribbling. Lois Faye Robinson, eight years old, her hair sprigged with a blue ribbon, leads the way to Sarah's house, her bare feet footnoting the worms' epic message. To her left and right are bipetaled blue dayflowers, like butterflies beside the road, and the smell of horsemint is all around her.

Sarah Grant is an eighty-six-year-old midwife. She lives in a blue-shuttered, earth-colored bungalow with a crippled cat, a dog, and a horse named Tillman. The bungalow is surrounded by small vegetable tracts, some outbuildings, and a leaning barn in which several dusty coffins are stacked. "My husband was the undertaker," Sarah says. "I brought them into the world and he took 'em out, as people used to say." Today Sarah spends her time in a faded white rocking chair on her tiny porch, warmed by the sun. Talking to Sarah is like assisting at a difficult delivery. It starts slowly but finally comes. Listening to the sound of her voice, you can hear her talking to all the women she has helped through childbirth—tones of assurance, strength, understanding, and joy.

"One hundred and forty," she says. "I think it's one hundred forty. I lost track. You can check the records at Bluffton—only two died. I started in 1932. The last—the last one was Ella Mae Stevens in January 1969. They go to the hospital in Savannah now and I ain't sorry a bit. They can do better at the hospital.

"The Lord and I do it together. People come and get me in a car or wagon. Sometimes I get there too late—the baby's waiting on me. First thing I do is cut the cord and tie it and dress it. Then I put the baby on a pallet. I wash his head and oil him all over—I don't wash the rest of him for two weeks. The baby comes in a "bed." There's another bed in the mother. Sometimes it doesn't come and you gotta get that bed out. Once the bed didn't come out for a week and I had to get the doctor—that's the only time the doctor came in thirty-seven years. When that bed comes you tend to the mother, then after that you tend to the baby. Then the mother nurses the baby. Sometimes there's no milk and we have to make a sugar teat. Yes, I think how they take the breast tells you something of the person they will be. But not all the time. Sometimes they are greedy when they start, but not later. Take Joe Bryan. He was a water baby. He was born on the water, in a boat. We were on the way to Savannah. I had everything with me. He came about half way over. We turned around and went right on back. He didn't cry—

too scared to cry. Some do come crying. Some come quiet. Some come fighting. Children don't be like they used to be. Used to be they'd keep their eyes shut for a long time. The children who come now look around with their eyes wide open. They got sense. Take the little Sullivan boy—he's the littlest one at the school now. He come like a dead child—limber. I gave him up for dead. But he didn't—a good while later he circulate about. He came foot foremost—when they come foot foremost they say he's going to be a wise fellow.

"I didn't use forceps, just my hands. Nothing else. Doctors use clamps and all kinds of things. Mine come by nature. Let it come by nature. Nature put it there—let nature bring it out. Let it come by nature. Sometimes the women do cry. Sometimes they get scared and cry. No, I don't give them drugs. I give them one pill to help them to go to sleep when it's all over."

Sarah went inside and brought out her tiny black leatherette bag, frayed at the edges. "I got this in Beaufort when I started in 1932," she said, unzipping the bag and taking out her surgical gown, folded neatly after her last birth in 1969. She placed it on top of the kit. "That's my gown, and those are my hand towels. That's my cotton. I got everything I need right here. My lysol, my soap, my handbrush. That's my tray to sterilize my scissors, and this is what I weigh the baby with." She held up a tiny, spring-operated scale. "That's my baby oil, that's my scissors, that's my eyedrops, and that's my eyedropper. This is my tape and paper to dress the baby's cord, and this is my pills. I give them one to take after they eat. We always give them ham and eggs, biscuits and grits and coffee after it was all over."

Folded in half at the very bottom of the black bag was Sarah's "Midwives Certificate of Registration," issued under the laws of the State of South Carolina for the year 1968. She proudly pointed to the back, where the "Rules and Regulations Governing Midwives in the State of South Carolina," were listed.

"I got ten dollars back then, in Beaufort when I started, and I had to split that between two of us. It got to be thirty dollars for me along by the time I quit, but it's worth more than that. It takes a lot of work. Some years you don't have none. Some years several. Some years you have five or six. They're all over, now. Some's in New York, some's in Miami, some's in Detroit."

Sarah enters her house, as neat inside as her midwife's kit. The kitchen, with its woodfired, cast iron, knuckle-footed stove ("Universal Stove, Rome Cooperative Foundry, Rome Georgia") is immaculate. Sarah busies herself there for a moment, then reappears on the porch, pushing the screen door open with her foot and carrying out a silver tray heavy with two cut-glass wine goblets and a bottle each of V.S.O.P. brandy and Samovar Vodka, with paper napkins folded into triangles and stuck between. "My brother gave me those wine glasses in 1913 for my wedding," she says. "He died of influenza at Camp Jackson during the First World War. He gave me six. Three's left." The brandy is eight years old, but only about an inch is gone from the neck of the bottle. The liquid in the vodka bottle is purple.

"It's God's medicine," Sarah says. "We make it from the berries here on the island."

Whatever shall be said upon the Subject here, is all extracted from our *English Writers*, who are very numerous, and universally agree, that *Carolina*, and especially in its *Southern* Bounds, is the most amiable Country of the Universe: that Nature has not bless'd the World with any Tract, which can be preferable to it, that *Paradise* with all her Virgin Beauties, may be modestly suppos'd at most but equal to its Native Excellencies.

—Sir Robert Montgomery

7. Epilogue

We do not yet know Guale. We, the Europeans and the Africans, came or were brought here to erect an alien culture on the Georgia land, and for the past four hundred years we have been busy at the task. We built forts in the wilderness to shut out its nights, its creatures, and its people. We gathered courage, marched out of the forts, and drove away the "Indians," the people who knew the land, knew it and its creatures, its winds and rains, by their oldest names. "The only good Indian is a dead Indian," was a common slogan then; "The only good marsh is a dead marsh," is the tacit assumption now. We assimilated those Indians who survived, and their descendants are now as ignorant as the rest of us.

The first people took away with them the thing we must learn again: how to talk pleasantly with the earth. Guale is a good place for practicing. Here and there on the islands and the riverbanks of the Georgia coast live people who know the words. Good conversations require some listening. If we learn that skill again, the New World may be discovered at last.

The land has new proprietors; and will they ever know it well enough? Will they be able to value the earth not only for its products, its man-made triumphs, but for what it is? We are not so nearly on speaking terms with nature as we used to be. . . . The earth insists on its intentions, however men may interpret them. Unity and use is what it asks. And use is what may be missing. To the degree that we may become dissociated by our power to exploit from what it is we exploit, so our senses will become atrophied, our skills diminished, our earth-related vision hopelessly dimmed. Without a new equation in which natural and human need are together in eternal process and identity, we may be lost to one another, and starved of our inheritance.

—John Hay

Underlying the beauty of the spectacle there is meaning and significance.
It is the elusiveness of that meaning that haunts us, that sends us again and
again into the natural world where the key to the riddle is hidden. It sends us
back to the edge of the sea, where the drama of life played its first scene on earth
and perhaps even its prelude; where the forces of evolution are at work today,
as they have been since the appearance of what we know as life; and where the
spectacle of living creatures faced by the cosmic realities of their world
is crystal clear.

—RACHEL CARSON

Marsh grass and bird, Ossabaw (John Earl)

Friends of the Earth in the United States, and sister organizations of the same name in other countries, are working for the preservation, restoration, and more rational use of the earth. We urge people to make more intensive use of the branches of government that society has set up for itself. Within the limits of support given us, we try to represent the public's interest in the environment before administrative and legislative bodies and in court. We add to, and need, the diversity of the conservation front in its vital effort to build greater respect for the earth and its living resources, including man.

We lobby for this idea. We work closely with our sister organizations abroad, and with new and old conservation organizations here and abroad that have saved so much for all of us to work for.

We publish—books, like this, and in smaller format—because of our belief in the power of the book and also to help support ourselves. Our environmental newspaper is "Not Man Apart."

If the public press is the fourth estate, perhaps we are the fifth. We speak out for you; we invite your support.

Friends of the Earth Foundation, also in San Francisco, supports the work of Friends of the Earth and organizations like it with projects in litigation and in scientific research, literature, and education.

Publisher's Note: The book is set in Centaur and Arrighi by Mackenzie & Harris Inc., San Francisco. It was lithographed and bound by Arnoldo Mondadori Editore, Verona, on coated paper made by Cartiera Celdit and Bamberger Kaliko Fabrik. The design is by David Brower. The Layout is by Kenneth Brower.